I WANT ME BACK!

There's Sunshine Ahead

John E. Long, Jr.

BALBOA PRESS
A DIVISION OF HAY HOUSE

Copyright © 2017 John E. Long, Jr.

All rights reserved. No part of this book may be used or reproduced by any means, graphic, electronic, or mechanical, including photocopying, recording, taping or by any information storage retrieval system without the written permission of the author except in the case of brief quotations embodied in critical articles and reviews.

Balboa Press books may be ordered through booksellers or by contacting:

Balboa Press
A Division of Hay House
1663 Liberty Drive
Bloomington, IN 47403
www.balboapress.com
1 (877) 407-4847

Because of the dynamic nature of the Internet, any web addresses or links contained in this book may have changed since publication and may no longer be valid. The views expressed in this work are solely those of the author and do not necessarily reflect the views of the publisher, and the publisher hereby disclaims any responsibility for them.

The author of this book does not dispense medical advice or prescribe the use of any technique as a form of treatment for physical, emotional, or medical problems without the advice of a physician, either directly or indirectly. The intent of the author is only to offer information of a general nature to help you in your quest for emotional and spiritual well-being. In the event you use any of the information in this book for yourself, which is your constitutional right, the author and the publisher assume no responsibility for your actions.

Any people depicted in stock imagery provided by Thinkstock are models, and such images are being used for illustrative purposes only.
Certain stock imagery © Thinkstock.

Print information available on the last page.

ISBN: 978-1-5043-6612-0 (sc)
ISBN: 978-1-5043-6614-4 (hc)
ISBN: 978-1-5043-6613-7 (e)

Library of Congress Control Number: 2016915331

Balboa Press rev. date: 12/30/2016

Contents

Prologue vii

Underdogs 1

How do I Know My Marriage is Over? 3

Before Telling Your Spouse You Want a Divorce 19

Divorce Law and Lawyers 39

Bad Behavior and the Indignity of Abuse 45

Physical Divorce 58

Emotional Divorce 74

Parenting 97

Integrity 120

Why I Can't Help Every Client 124

PROLOGUE

"If your life were a movie – where did you go wrong?"

My clients tell me that question is one of the most effective things I ask them. It's so simple and so important. In "The Movie of Your Life," what role are you playing? Which character are you?

I've been many characters and played many roles in my movie – I've been "The Drunkard" and "The Teatotaler", "The Cheater" and "The Cheated", and depending on which one of my children you ask, I've been "World's Best Dad" and "World's Worst Dad"!

But my most constant role has been "The Underdog". I didn't know I was an underdog until someone pointed it out to me. It happened during a life-altering confrontation in January 1961 – my first week of law school.

"Long?!"

I heard a formidable voice booming across the walkway outside the law library. I turned and observed Professor Daniel Murray looking in my direction. We'd never met personally, but I recognized him as my professor from *Legal Research and Writing*.

As I approached, he asked, "Are you Long?" "Yes, Sir."

Without hesitating, he said, "Well I don't think you'll be with us for long."

Needless to say, I was stunned.

It took me a few moments to absorb what he was saying. The introduction and admonition overwhelmed me.

Standing before him with my arms full of casebooks and study materials, I felt as if he'd just punched me in the gut. I was frozen as I contemplated his words.

As he started to walk away I somehow managed to speak.

"Professor, before you flunk me out, is there anything I can do to salvage my law school education?"

He stopped and pondered my question. "You have the lowest LSAT score in the entire law school which means your reading skills are woefully deficient, and you will never be able to keep up with the work. It would be wise to go visit the academic counseling center on the undergraduate campus and register for an aptitude test which would measure your vocabulary, comprehension and speed reading ability." He walked away before I could say another word.

I jammed my books in a locker and raced across campus to register for the exam. I took the test the following day and returned for the results shortly thereafter.

"Mr. Long, I regret to inform you that your scores indicate a below average competency for your current position as a first-year law student," the proctor advised. She sat me down and revealed my results. "You have the vocabulary of a sophomore in college, the reading comprehension of an eleventh grader, and you speed read at the level of a fifth grader."

Although stunned and demoralized, I asked, "Can you save me?"

"Mr. Long, I can only help you save yourself. If you put in the hard work and time, you will have a fighting chance."

"Okay," I said. "I'll do whatever it takes."

"It won't be easy, Mr. Long. I'll need to tutor you an hour a day, five days a week for the next sixteen weeks. It will cost $600."

I phoned my father that night for assistance, and I was most fortunate to receive it. Sixteen weeks later I retested. I attained a senior in college level in all three categories. I also took my first semester law school exams that week and passed them all.

Before parting ways for the summer, my friends and I decided to lunch together one last time on the law school picnic tables. Just as I bit into my sandwich, I felt a tap on my shoulder.

"May I have a word with you, Mr. Long?" It was Professor Murray. I jumped up and followed him to a shady spot under one of the Royal Poinciana trees that dot the University of Miami campus.

"You owe me, young man." Professor Murray had heard about my exam results as well as my retest scores at the academic counseling center. "I'd like you to address next year's incoming class during fall orientation. I want you to tell them your story."

I agreed, although it was the last thing I wanted to do. I didn't want to share my humiliating story of remedial tutoring to dig myself out of fifth-grade level competency. But I was so grateful for Professor Murray, and didn't want to start letting him down now.

"See you in September, Long."

My first marriage ended three weeks later.

Movies look different when you watch in slow motion. You notice more details, more scenery. Replays, particularly those in slow motion, are capable of showing you what you missed the first time around. You can also be surprised to find moments which characterize an entire life yet lived.

When I arrived at the auditorium that September morning of 1961, the room was full of excited, nervous new law students. While I waited for my turn at the podium in a seat in the last row of the theater, I went over what I'd say.

Watching the scene play out, I see an uncertain 23-year-old kid, anxious about what he would say and how he'd be judged. I see myself quickly describing the nuts and bolts of what had to be done to avoid failure – the endless hours in the library, the tutoring, and the weekend practice drills. I don't see where I revealed the one thing that mattered most – *my unwillingness to give up on myself.* I suppose I didn't know that lesson yet.

When I left the auditorium that morning, I had no idea what lay ahead in my life. I was just a kid from Long Island, newly average – an underdog full of wonder. As I walked to the post office to mail my first monthly child support payment, I had no idea it was only the first of 348, or that I'd fail another wife and other innocent children.

The hope of my youth enveloped me on that sidewalk. I didn't know that the easiest fights in my life were behind me. I simply wondered *who would I become? Would I be able to make a difference and help people? Who would I meet along the way?*

This underdog was in for quite an adventure…

Henry

It all started with Henry. Henry invited my wife and I to dinner to celebrate the finality of his divorce. We joined Henry and his financial advisor, Bert, at a restaurant in town. As expected, we had a fantastic evening. Henry was always full of wonderful stories and great humor.

I was shocked when he suddenly announced to the table that I should write a book and help others as he believed I had helped him. I thought it was one of the most ridiculous ideas I'd ever heard. Me? Write a book? What do I have to say that isn't already being said? But Henry insisted.

As clients go, he was one of my most fun surprises. Henry hired me after his wife announced she was leaving him. During his first consultation, I confronted him with my belief that damaged self-esteem was at the core of his marital demise, and recovering his self-worth was as important as preserving his enormous net worth.

He took a deep breath and leaned back into the leather Chesterfield sofa in my office.

After a few moments of pondering, he looked down at his lap. We sat in silence as Henry considered the proposition. He finally looked up and said, "Jack, you're right."

Henry was a wonderful surprise because most men in his position – extraordinarily wealthy, successful, and "dumped", are the least likely to admit their self-esteem isn't what it should be. My message is hard for them to accept because men like Henry usually derive their ego, or false sense of self-esteem, by connecting it to their net worth. They prefer looking at what's on the outside, toys, homes, bank accounts, cars, etc., to value who they are. It's especially difficult for wealthy men to accept the truth that their self-esteem is damaged when the one thing they fear becomes painfully obvious in divorce – their wives probably only married for money.

If there were ever a woman who married a man for money, it was Henry's wife. She was the grand poobah of gold-digging. She made no effort to conceal her motives and wasn't shy about going after every last penny. She hired one of the most aggressive, junkyard dog attorneys in town and got to work. Some of her requests included an excessive allowance per month for clothing, food and entertainment, a new Bentley, and thousands per month for veterinary bills for her hairball-hacking cat, a Himalayan Persian who wore a diamond tennis bracelet as a pet collar.

Henry's wealth came mostly from successes in commercial real estate. He made millions selling vast tracks of land to a Fortune 500 company who then developed the land.

Even though Henry was finally able to see his wife for the marauding, materialistic, money-grubbing mite she really was, he still was willing to give in to her requests. I explained to Henry that I couldn't stand by and allow his low self-esteem to dictate financial decisions which would deplete his estate.

I told him he was not standing up for himself, and if he really wanted to restore his lost self-esteem and divorce with dignity, he needed to begin finding the strength to stand up for his rights.

Henry worked hard to hold onto his bank accounts as his wife harassed him and did everything possible to try and empty them the way she'd already done with much of his self-esteem. She tried all her usual manipulative tricks to force Henry into giving her what she wanted, including sexual favors. Though Henry was tempted several times to give in to her requests, he slowly regained his self-esteem by sticking to the suggestions I'd given, and honoring his commitment to divorce with dignity.

Henry wasn't surprising because he ended up with a renewed purpose, restored self-worth, or far more of his assets than he could've imagined – he was a surprise because I didn't expect a man like him to be one of the first to think my message of damaged self-esteem worthy of becoming a book.

For years, I'd received letters from former clients thanking me for helping them recover their self-esteem during divorce. I'd always been overwhelmed by their gratitude and insistence that I was the one who helped them restore their self-worth and find happiness again. But not until several months after that dinner with Henry, did the letters start mentioning me writing a book to share my philosophy about why self-esteem is the root of all marital dissatisfaction and divorce. Whenever the idea of a book was mentioned I always thought the same thing – Aren't there all kinds of books on the market which discuss this? What would make my book so special? How would it be any different than the others? So I shrugged off the inquiries, and my assistant filed away the messages.

I finally began to seriously consider the idea in 2008. I discussed it with close family, a few friends, and some former clients. I explained my concerns about never having been trained as a psychologist or marriage counselor. My beliefs were formulated from years as a divorce attorney, my experiences as a husband and father, and plain old common sense – was I even qualified to write a book? They encouraged me that my common sense, life experience, and career were exactly what made my advice so useful. They insisted that it go into a book.

After consulting with psychotherapists, writers, and clients, and researching marriage and divorce self-help materials, I discovered there was something missing from the market. I noticed there are few books written about the proper philosophical approach to *divorcing with dignity* and the significance of recovering your self-worth during divorce. Most books provide general information about the clinical approach, or "how-to" divorce. This information is available on Google and in mainstream publications and books. Nothing was really telling people what they needed to find out… how to "get themselves back". It also occurred to me that most of the books out there repeat information which can be found elsewhere. There isn't anyone else writing from the inside out…no insiders of the divorce profession telling you how to survive with your most important asset intact – your self-esteem.

The reason why recovering your self-esteem in divorce is crucial is because our feelings about ourselves is the one thing in the world which can't be taken away from us unless we let that happen. When we confuse our self-esteem with tangible, external items that have no value other than that which is ascribed to us by others, such as boats, cars, homes, etc., those things become a substitute for ourselves. We think that we are worth what they are worth, and the risk of losing any of that in a divorce is overwhelming and terrifying. Who are you when these things fade, or are spent, or are lost in a divorce or elsewhere? Can you recover? What is your "worth" without them? This is what makes divorce so frightening for so many – they judge themselves on these tangible, external objects, and when faced with the threat of losing them, they truly believe they could "lose everything."

For example, men seek wealth and power to attract beautiful women, and women seek beauty to attract wealthy men.

Who are they when this stuff goes away? They don't know, and they have nothing to fall back on, no identity apart from that which can be lost in an instant. So they end up in divorce court, looking to hold onto what defines them.

Without that self-awareness, fear and insecurity grip them, and there is no room to focus on anything but winning the battle of net worth during their divorce. This low self-esteem and lack of self-awareness drives the intense bitterness and fury of the dissolution process.

THE BIG QUESTION: "Jack, this message about self-worth and net worth sounds good, but I'm not interested if you're suggesting that I must sacrifice one for the other. I have too much to lose in this divorce financially. Can't I just focus on that now and then come back to self-esteem recovery later?"

I know just where you're at right now. I've been in your shoes twice as a married man and once as a partner in a failed 10 year relationship. I've represented over 5,000 divorcing clients during my 51 years of practice. I get it. You're looking at this book the same way I looked at the proctor in

Miami, asking "Can you save me?" Most of you fear the failure that can come with losing your net worth and assets, and want me to tell you how to avoid that. I will.

But you first need to know what you're really terrified about. You are really terrified that whatever happens in a divorce or potential divorce, will drive you so low, either financially, emotionally, psychologically, mentally or socially, and the failure will be so complete, that you'll never, ever recover.

The premise of this book is that the root of marital demise and divorce is a damaged or depleted self-esteem of one or both spouses. It's been at the core of every case I've ever handled, and once I confront my clients about this, most agree. But beyond that basic common denominator, I also observed other links between each case and my own personal divorce experiences:

- Everyone facing divorce wants to know, "Is divorce really better for me than staying married?"
- "How do I know the marriage is over?"
- "Am I going to be pushed so low and lose so much that I won't ever recover?"

What lies at the heart of all of these concerns is the same, and it's what lies at the heart of a fear of failure.....the fear that you'll not be able to get back up. It's the fear that you won't survive the loss.

When your self-esteem isn't where it should be, it's because you've bought into the opinions of others. You allow them to determine your worth, your goals, your choices and your "lovability". You lose a sense of who you really are. I hear this over and over again with clients who tell me, "Jack, I lost who I am and I want me back."

So it's no wonder that as you're considering divorce, you feel insecure about whether you are making the right decisions to guarantee you will be okay, let alone happy. How can you know what to do or how to do it when you don't trust your judgment? Whose judgment should you trust?

I completely understand where you are, and this book will get you the answers you need to recover your self-worth and get the best net worth settlement you can. But what winning the battle of self-worth gets you what no other battle can, is the ability to not only get back up from the failure and recover, but also the knowledge of how to recover better than ever so you can surpass who you were when you first fell down.

It took many years and many failures for me to finally learn this lesson myself. It wasn't until I hit rock bottom in 1978 that I began to open my eyes and find the courage to watch my life from the outside in. I started to watch what was happening around and within me. I needed to understand where I went wrong and why. Only then would I be able to learn from my mistakes and take responsibility for my life. I needed to see who I was, change what I didn't like, and understand why I'd made bad choices.

The eyes of my mind began to open. I began to see the similarities between my life and my past decisions, and my clients' lives and their past decisions. The more I understood of myself and my clients, the better I got at interpreting both my movie and theirs. I saw the causes behind the effects. In my office, the effects were divorce, and the causes were typically one or more of the usual suspects – abuse, infidelity, control, money, alcoholism, and the "we grew apart" concept. My personal patterns and disasters were so similar to theirs. I was on my way to discovering that the common denominator among all my divorcing clients and myself was a damaged self-esteem of one or both spouses.

My path to recovering the self-esteem I'd lost and repairing the self-inflicted damage of my life was painfully rocky, but it was paramount to my personal and professional growth.

Rebuilding my damaged self-esteem enabled me to shed my ego and evolve beyond my insecurities. More importantly, I let go of my unwillingness to be seen as the person I really am. Once I got in touch with who I was and began the process of changing the things I saw that I didn't like, I was freed to see others as they were.

In 1981, I met the most inspiring, courageous, and resolute client I've ever represented. She was divorcing a brutally abusive man. It was agonizing to listen to her stories and watch her suffer from the consequences of his grotesque dysfunction. Her strength and grace astonished me. Her divorce was finalized in 1985, and four years later, I married her. I'd failed twice in marriage but once I married again in 1989, she secured my future as a successful husband, and dramatically improved my ability to serve clients.

My success in life and in law has been co-mingled, and my success in one area led to more success in the other.

Likewise, the failures in each helped me improve in each. Without my wife, I never would have become aware that spouses must nurture each other's self-esteem and pay attention to it within themselves, and within the marriage. My wife constantly pours wisdom into me and nurtures my self-esteem on a daily basis. I learned how important this was, and when I began to apply what I was learning and truly nurture her, I knew I was on to something.

And this is where my path diverged from other attorneys. I paid attention to my movie and the clients' movies, and I learned the big, meaningful, life-changing lessons. I learned from watching all the movies, and applied the lessons from each to the other. That's why my practice has been so enriched and blessed – I paid attention to the show. And I taught the lessons of their lives long after their case was over and they found new happiness all over again. This is what I fear other divorce attorneys are missing.....they aren't watching and learning. When I saw damaged self-esteem was the root of the divorce phenomenon, not only was I willing to act, I was able to take the necessary steps.

My approach to divorce law evolved into what I call a "clinical-humanistic hybrid". All aspects of the client's needs are addressed, as long as the client is receptive to that approach. I explain that the clinical part of the representation is my resolution of the equitable distribution issues, alimony, parenting plans, etc. The clinical aspects include everything that a client expects to receive from a divorce attorney. But my approach goes beyond treating the clinical issues at stake in a divorce process. It addresses the hidden, underlying, difficult emotional causes of the marital demise. But not every client is receptive to the humanistic component of my philosophy. Yet this hybrid approach is flexible and adaptive, and I'm able to tailor the representation as necessary.

Most clients are receptive however, and sadly and reluctantly agree that they want their self-esteem back after making this admission. And I don't take it lightly when they do – it means they trust me to guide them both clinically and emotionally. This is an exceptionally difficult period in their lives, and they are at their most vulnerable. It's my obligation as an attorney, and as a decent human being, to respect their journey, assist them in the process, and ensure they're acting in their best interest, as best I can.

My hybrid approach is distinctive in one other way – as I help my clients regain their self-esteem and restore their dignity, I'm able to see them for who they really are, but I can only do that once I show them who I really am. I use my own stories with my clients to the extent it will help.

This is why the book is partly autobiographical – it's one component of my style that's enabled my clients to recover. My clients tell me by sharing the brutal truth of my past and my mistakes, it disarms them and negates any fear they have of me judging them.

Disclosing my own sins and personal failures allows them to feel safe enough to meet me in the raw honesty of that moment. They are able to see me as a real person. They can look beyond the business suit and tie, the board certifications, and the diplomas and see that my mistakes have been just as bad as theirs, and often worse. There's a connection once I share how I've made the same awful choices and suffered the same hideous consequences. An understanding develops, and they know I'm rooting for them – something that has tremendous power when clients with depleted self-esteem have no ability to even root for themselves.

Rooting for yourself is crucial for redemption. You must believe that where you are now is not where you need to be forever. Life is like a movie and the scenes from your past don't have to dictate the scenes ahead. But you need help figuring out how to avoid repeating the same old scripts, how to re-cast, and how to be a better character in "The Movie of Your Life". The secret is that beginning the recovery of your self-worth is what makes the rest easier, and sets you up for the most priceless gift divorce can bring – the happiness that comes with "getting you back".

How do you "get you back" when you don't know who you are, where you are, and are terrified about what's happening? I'll give you a road map. You are about to undertake a difficult and complicated but very rewarding journey – you are looking for you. It's like a little treasure buried under the dirt and filth of what happened in your marriage. Life is an adventure, and there's no doubt divorce can be the most turbulent adventure of all, but I can help you find the treasure at the end. Just commit to the hard work and refuse to give up – the treasure is far too precious to walk away from.

I believe in the treasure. I want people to find it in themselves and their marriages before it's too late. I've often been frustrated by my inability to get the message out before it was too late, before the client appeared in my office unwilling to attempt reconciliation. How does one get this message out to anyone before it's too late? I'm hoping this book might help. But I'm not convinced it will. I'm worried because it doesn't fit into any categories recognized by modern booksellers or book markets. Its part memoir, part "how-to" divorce, part self-help, and part autobiographical. It doesn't fit into neat, orderly, recognized categories. It's too much like life – like my life – like my clients' lives.

It Was Always the Clients

If Central Casting was choosing my clients, they sure picked some doozies. I've represented all kinds of maniacs, miscreants, rascals, rapscallions, cross-dressers, transgressors, imps, pimps, wimps, weasels, CEOs, SOBs, heroes, zeroes, wackos, billionaires, beauty queens, doormats, dumb asses, jackasses, boozers, losers, church ladies, trophy wives, tough guys, swingers – and presumably one international hit man. This array is the exception, not the rule, since most of my clients were good human beings.

All of them, from top to bottom, from sinner to saint, shared one thing – they were excellent teachers. In truth, I've had some of the most spectacular clients an attorney could hope for. My life has been enriched by them all – even the ones I didn't like, and the ones who fired me. When I became a lawyer, I expected a lifetime of serving those who needed help, making a meaningful difference where and when I could. What I didn't expect was what happened instead – the clients served me. The real blessings came from being served myself.

Past clients help present clients, and this book includes many client letters and stories. This book is written in their honor. I've just been the conduit for their lessons. It was just a theory. But you believed and legitimized my message. You needed someone to show you exactly what to do and how to do it. Many of you even needed to know exactly what to say and when to say it. Together we learned from each other. And while I still have a voice and can make a difference beyond the four walls of my office, it's time to share our stories, lessons, laughs, failures and sweet successes. So this book is for anyone who is interested in salvaging their self-esteem.

It took me a while to understand my ability to overcome in life was based on one thing – a belief in my own redemption. And I went after it. It didn't matter a professor counted me out, or a school, or even the State of New York when I failed the bar exam for the first time. I knew the truth – I might have been down, but I wasn't out.

Sure, I started off just like you, desperately looking for someone else to save me. But no tutor, no proctor, no divorce lawyer, or "perfect spouse" can ever save you. You must save yourself. And it's hard work. You have to work when you don't want to, in your spare time, and on the weekends.

Whatever has happened in your life thus far, you never lose the opportunity to choose which character you will play, or what the next scene in your movie will be. You just need a small glimmer of faith in yourself to act.

So here's the question – when will your redemption scene start? What catastrophe must occur in your life to force you into action? If it's not divorce, what will it be? How deep a disaster must occur before you let yourself break and rebuild?

Chapter 1

Underdogs

One of the most common statements I hear from clients is "I want me back." Isn't that what you really want back too?

It's hard to think that you have a shot at getting yourself back. You feel like such a failure. You've already lost many important things, including your self-respect, self-confidence, and security. You don't know what lies ahead for you – and it's terrifying. You might be facing the possibility of losing your house, your money, and even your dignity if the divorce gets nasty.

You feel like the least likely person on earth to make a comeback. You are the underdog. Welcome to the club.

When you are the underdog because of divorce and damaged self-esteem, you feel like no one champions you. You are undervalued, an unlikely victor. Underdogs don't win or lose because of how others perceive them, or value them. They win because their opinion of their ability to succeed comes from within. They refuse to give up on themselves.

At the beginning of the divorce process, you are already so low, so defeated. And the anxiety about who will get what in the settlement can be overwhelming. You don't want to "fail" in that respect either. But if you only adhere to the clinical approach of divorce, the nuts and bolts of property distribution, parenting plans, etc., and ignore the psychological issues of divorce, you will fail again.

The best movies have it all, tragedy and triumph, heartbreak and love. They all share the common elements of suffering and overcoming. When faced with dramatic obstacles and loss, the adversity thrusts the protagonist into what's known as the "character arc". The arc accelerates maturity and growth, but only when the choice to fight for victory is made. The best movie heroes and memorable characters aren't the ones who let the sword lie – but rather, in their weakest hour, bend down and grab hold, facing the unknown with courage and commitment. They fight for their redemption.

Please pick up the sword. In this book, I'm giving you the tools you need to overcome, the clinical tools and the humanistic tools. I'm handing you scripts, and feeding you the lines. Do you have the courage to follow?

And that's what lies beneath my cast of characters. I've always been the underdog. Granted, there were times when I've been the underdog that no one roots for. We're all underdogs if we want to be – or we hide at home with our head under the covers.

Chapter 2

How do I Know My Marriage is Over?

Most people contemplating divorce look for assurance that their decision, whatever it may be, will bring them happiness and peace. This is why there are so many websites and books on this very topic. It's big business to give people what they want from a guide to help them make this significant decision. They are looking for a guide which makes them feel secure in the knowledge that it's "the secret" to deciding whether to divorce. After making this decision for myself twice, and after seeing thousands of clients struggle with it as well, I can tell you the one thing I know for sure – nothing worth having comes free, and the most important part of this decision-making process is putting in the work to find your answer.

People need a guide that makes them accountable and doesn't let them off the hook. The only way to find peace with your decision to divorce is by accepting personal responsibility for the decision. My guide to determining whether your marriage is over applies to everyone, no matter what condition your self-esteem is, or what kind of a spouse you have. This is because, if you've been in a marriage that has damaged your self-esteem, or you feel uncertain about how to reach the decision to stay or go, this section of the book is for you. Feeling uncertain is common, and I think it's a good thing. It means you're giving the decision to divorce the attention and consideration it deserves. It is not something that should be casually entered into. The decision is complex with endless consequences to consider.

Most significantly, divorce breaks up a family. Beyond that, there are many challenging psychological, emotional and financial repercussions resulting from divorce. If you honestly know there is no acceptable alternative to divorce, you will implicitly have peace in your heart. There will be no need to justify anything. Justification is like rationalization. People engage in rationalization to make excuses for their behavior, actions and decisions. If you truly cannot find one acceptable alternative to divorce that allows you to honor your dignity and integrity, and rebuild your self-esteem, there's no need for a single excuse. That is not an excuse. That is an eyes wide open, well-considered, pronouncement of what is and what is not acceptable in your life. It declares what you will and will not tolerate, excuse, or ignore in your life from now on. This is about your honor.

If you aren't guarding your honor, who is? Honestly being able to say that to yourself requires that you can't harbor any secret thoughts such as "well, maybe if I tried counseling…", or "gee, if I tried to sit down and explain why I'm so unhappy, maybe…"

No. If you have these secret whispers in your ear as you ask yourself this question, you will not find peace about your decision in the long run. The last thing you want is to look back and wonder if you made the right decision, particularly if you have children. You must exhaust all possible avenues of restoration, correction, forgiveness, therapy, communication, and love.

You know it's over when you can honestly say this sentence to yourself, and feel at peace after you say it:

> ***"I cannot find one acceptable alternative to divorce which allows me to honor my dignity and integrity, and rebuild my self-esteem."***

You, not Aunt Ethel, not your drinking buddy Marty, not your overbearing mother or your outspoken, loud-mouthed friends – you are the only one who can make the decision because you are truly the only one who can answer it based on ALL the evidence and ALL the circumstances.

Many people end their marriages in haste. They are so consumed by resentment and frustration, and their emotions dictate this life-altering decision. The best way to decide to divorce is to use all your resources, not just your emotions and heart, but also your head and your spirit. Often, people only rely on their emotions when contemplating divorce.

It's easy to say "well, we fell out of love", or "I just don't love her anymore". That is a preposterous reason to divorce. That's like saying "I married him because I liked him". There has to be more to it than that in order for the decision to work out successfully.

So, once you aren't relying strictly on your emotions, you have to look elsewhere for certainty and clues as to whether the marriage can be salvaged. It is a decision that should require sacrifices – you must do what you do not want to do in order to be certain there is nothing else to do besides divorcing. This means you have to look at your marriage and your life and evaluate what options exist for improvement. You must see how you yourself can make changes which will positively affect your marriage. This is not the time to blame your spouse or underestimate what he or she might be capable of in order to save the marriage.

What is an "acceptable alternative" to divorce? It depends, and the answer is different for every couple. But when you are steadfast in your commitment to having a marriage where your integrity, dignity and self-esteem can be honored, you're one step closer to recognizing the one acceptable alternative when you find it.

Let's face it, if you're far enough along on the contemplation of the divorce journey, you are secretly hoping that this script will lead you to the conclusion that divorce is the only option. You are the dumper. You are miserable and tired of being in a marriage where you feel undervalued, underappreciated and unloved. You might even think you don't like your spouse at all anymore, and wonder why you married in the first place. So you are ready for happiness and relief. You want that golden ticket to Happy Town.

You need to get real. Searching for one acceptable alternative is not going to be like a journey where you suddenly stumble upon a magic carpet that will solve all your problems. The word is "acceptable" not perfect or wonderful. This part is about paying your fare for the ticket to Happy Town.

Divorce is a radical and complete disunification of what was once completely united. It means to sever, dissociate, dissolve the matrimonial bonds, disconnect, detach, break apart. Divorcing someone disgorges the mutual responsibilities shared by each spouse. There are no unsaid expectations or obligations that entitle you to hold a grudge or build resentment about. It is "The End". Final. Fini. Over. You're on your own. Free.

But are you really ready to be on your own? Are you ready to be free?

People who tell you that when they first seriously entertained the idea of divorce, it sounded good, are lying. I don't care how bad their marriage is or what their circumstance. People don't like the idea of divorcing their spouse upon first consideration. It's a terrifying proposition, emotionally, financially, etc. Everybody considering divorce, the dumpers and the dumpees, all share the same fear and wonder – *what will happen to me*?

This is why divorce is so terrifying at first. At least when you're in a marriage, even a bad marriage, you feel more secure because there are "two of you against the world". You have a partner who will at least bear witness to your life, and purportedly look out for you and help you when you need help. But this safety goes away in divorce.

Many spouses, especially those with low self-esteem, feel they aren't ready to go out on their own. They don't trust their ability to survive outside of marriage.

When I was considering divorce from my first two wives, these thoughts ran through my mind, although I was mostly concerned about what would happen to my children. This is an even scarier proposition because it's bad enough to feel like you're ruining your own life, let alone the lives of your innocent children. So how does one overcome these fears and move into a space where divorce becomes an option despite the endless "what ifs"?

With so many people in miserable marriages these days, I'm not surprised when I hear a client tell me the divorce was a breeze compared to the marriage. When two people are already separated in heart or mind, much of the loss and grieving is over.

When faced with these unknown variables, it's difficult to get an accurate "preview" of "The Movie of Your Life" after the divorce. This is what makes choosing divorce so tough. Life is all about making choices and responding to the cards you're dealt. When you review "The Movie of Your Life", you see that many cards are not of our own choosing but we spend our life trying to respond properly and learn important lessons from the mistakes we make along the way. But, choosing to divorce is a card we draw ourselves. And it's a big card. How can we possibly select it when we aren't sure of the consequences, and blame for the selection lies solely with ourselves? At least if we don't choose the divorce card and stay in the marriage, we can control the outcome of our movie – there is security and comfort in sticking to the script and anticipating that the scenes of tomorrow will look about the same as those from yesterday and today.

Thoughtfully considering divorce requires you to imagine what "The Movie of Your Life" would look like in either scenario, divorce or no divorce. The best way to do this is to evaluate the variables, the known and unknown, and consider how you'd fare based on the resources you either have right now, or can acquire with time. For instance, money issues are a major concern for most divorcing couples and divorce typically causes each spouse to lose one of two things – substantial portions of net worth, or access to a spouse's income or other assets. But until the final decree, the financial settlement is an unknown variable (unless you have a valid pre or post-nuptial agreement).

So when you look ahead at your movie, should you remain married, the money variable is much more predictable than if you were to divorce. But by looking at the laws of your State to get a general idea of what each spouse is financially entitled to, and calculating your total assets and liabilities, and considering what resources you have to secure income independently after a divorce, you can better anticipate how that divorce movie will look. This is what I mean by using the resources you do have to predict the variables. Do you have any skills or training to secure a job and gain income post-divorce? What can you do now to prepare for that option? Do you need to go back to school or take a few computer classes to brush up on office technology?

A lot of people who think about the cost of returning to work or consider the financial loss associated with most divorces, get turned off and resign themselves to staying in the marriage. They literally "count the cost" of divorce and conclude divorce is too expensive. Obviously, this happens frequently when considering the impact of divorce on children, social lives, physical changes, etc. The "Divorce Movie" simply looks too hard and too expensive. But that's actually a positive thing. It means they've at least considered what the movie would be, and can thoughtfully decide to stay in the marriage. That's the result of proactive, thorough and diligent divorce contemplation. By working through my guide you will arrive at a conclusion with your eyes wide open and the process will dignify your decision.

While everyone who first considers divorce faces the big fear of "what will happen to me?", those with the lowest self-esteem are often unable to look through the long-term lens, or when they do, miss the hopefulness of that lens. If the turbulence and challenge of the short-term view is frightening, it's usually because the ability to cope with the challenges tips the scale in favor of clinging to the spouse and scuttling the idea of divorce.

Or things might not look scary through the short-term lens, but a look at the movie through the long-term lens is devoid of hope or happiness. It's hard to imagine the long-term positive repercussions of divorce, if you don't believe you deserve better than what you currently endure in the marriage.

Spouses with such damaged self-esteem believe leaving the marriage might jeopardize their survival, and even if they have every possible resource to compensate for the unknown variables, they are all worthless because they aren't mentally or emotionally strong enough to apply those resources successfully or effectively. When I see clients like this, it is painful to see how their self-imposed handicap truly paralyzes them.

My theory is that most marriages fall apart because of the damaged self-esteem of one or both spouses, but since my clients have proven that divorcing spouses are unaware of the self-esteem disease, something else must be driving couples to stay together, even as they slowly sacrifice pieces of who they are for their spouse and the marriage.

At the root of this realization is the unavoidable, harsh fact that there's no such thing as a spouse who doesn't disappoint. How frequently or how deep the disappointment depends on each spouse, and is different in every marriage, but I've seen thousands of clients who all treat the hurt of disappointment the same. They use money. Eleanor was a brave client who was very receptive to my self-esteem message, and as she progressed through the divorce, her personal transformation was astonishing.

Eleanor

"My husband cheated throughout our entire marriage, and I happily lived in denial. It was so much easier not to face it. I focused on raising our children, and when they all went off to college, I was alone in our enormous home for the first time."

"Even when he was home, we could go for hours without speaking or seeing each other – he lived in his study, and I was always upstairs in my dressing room. I knew he was cheating, but I wasn't ready to face it and confront him because divorce was too scary. The risk of losing my home, my lavish shopping sprees, my fancy cars, and my fantastic vacations with girlfriends was too much to bear."

"But when the market collapsed and our business failed, the money I used to soothe myself and compensate for the agony of his infidelity evaporated. Losing the money freed me from the self-imposed prison, and I finally saw what he'd seen all along – that as long as his money flowed in, it was a tool to keep me controlled, quiet about the infidelity, maintaining his image of the perfect wife with the perfect house. I am so grateful that your self-esteem message empowered me to see the truth. I'm so much better now. I know that money can't control me anymore. He can no longer put a price on me and use money to absolve guilt."

Not every client is like Eleanor in terms of money as the soother. Many times, clients stay married for the children. I know of some cases where a husband was threatening the wife with losing custody and access to the children if she dared to leave the marriage. A situation like that is exceptionally agonizing, dysfunctional, abusive and challenging. My hope for those in a similar scenario is that you can either find a successful way out soon, or work on building your self-esteem and plan a way out once your children turn 18. Please find the courage to look ahead to what your post-divorce movie life can be, and use everything you've got to make it happen.

Some people are enchanted with the "freedom" concept, but are either too lazy to make it happen, or unwilling for other reasons. Then there are some who like the comfort and security the bonds of marriage provide, legally and otherwise. They like having someone responsible for them, and think it's too much trouble to be bothered with divorce and its repercussions. They figure as long as their spouse stays out of their way, and they are married strangers who don't bother each other, it's worth staying married because you can do what you want and not worry about it. They might also be the least prepared or least resourced to begin life without their spouse.

Some people are much more tempted to divorce, and are enchanted with the "freedom" the concept of divorce offers. These are the spouses who look at divorce through the short-term lens, but sometimes peek through the long-term one.

They can catch glimpses of what a future after divorce might look like, but when they consider the cost, they decide it isn't worth it, or at least isn't worth it yet.

But many others evolve. This evolution might begin when they start asking themselves modified versions of what they previously asked. The question no longer is "Do I trust myself to survive on my own?" It becomes "Do I trust myself to survive if I stay?" Something shifts in their minds, and they start looking beyond the short-term terror of ending a marriage, and look into long-term possibilities.

Freedom fighters are those who can work through that fear and dare to see what lies beyond the short-term to evaluate their decision.

The point is that you see divorce for what it is – a final, irrevocable severance of the marital union. It doesn't mean you can't still be friends or co-parent. But it does mean that the scene changes in your movie – there is a recasting.

Will you allow yourself to act in order to pursue recovery of your self-esteem? And second, will your spouse allow you to do what's necessary to rebuild and recover, when it necessitates a renegotiation of roles and shifts the marital dynamic?

I don't mean to sound harsh, but why bother pondering divorce if you aren't interested in living a life of dignity and integrity, one in which you feel good about yourself? If that's not what you want, and you already are missing it within the marriage, then what makes you think divorce will solve your unhappiness? Aren't you considering divorce because you are unhappy and don't want to be unhappy anymore? Do you really believe getting away from your spouse will make any difference if you don't commit to doing the work of finding happiness and peace? Since when has loss guaranteed happiness? Getting away from your spouse might help, but at most, it's only a 50 percent improvement.

Allowing: Nancy and Michael
Would Nancy allow Michael to improve his self-esteem within the marriage despite the changes it would necessitate in the dynamic? And would he be able to accept the changes in her and the results within the marriage? I had a feeling I'd find out sooner or later…

Shortly after my meeting with Michael, I was due in court. As I drove to the courthouse I thought about Michael and wondered if Nancy would be receptive to the self-esteem message. Would she agree they needed to pay attention and nurture each other's self-esteem in order to help the marriage? And if not, would she allow Michael to recover the self-esteem and dignity he's lost? I worried that I hadn't emphasized the challenges of the changing marital dynamic that would come from his or both of their growth.

I knew from my own and from my clients' experiences, that allowing yourself to recover and having a spouse allow you to recover is very tough. And it really is a two-part issue.

Until you accept the self-esteem message, you can't allow yourself to act…. you can't act on anything you don't believe. Second, if your spouse thinks it's nonsense, you are unlikely to get the space you need, and your spouse will not be able to adapt to the changes.

Michael and Nancy were able to survive because they both acknowledged the self-worth issues, and they both ALLOWED each other the space to grow and recover. For the self-worth of either to improve, let alone for the salvation of the marriage, it takes both partners to commit to renegotiating the marriage and also to providing the other with the proper environment and space, as well as emotional support.

So will you take advantage of the opportunity to grow? Allow is not a command – it means you have the choice or option to do something. No one is forcing you to recover what's been lost. It's your option to act. If you aren't willing or concerned about recovering your dignity, integrity and self-esteem, then why bother getting divorced?

Will you be "allowed" to recover what you've lost of yourself while staying in the marriage? Can your spouse tolerate and allow your growth and pursuit of living with enhanced dignity and integrity? Can the marriage be renegotiated to allow each of you to evolve and re-define your roles to strengthen your union? These are questions you might not know the answers to, and I believe you need to find out.

Let's be honest. Honoring yourself, your spouse, and your marriage is a constant struggle, and no one ever does it perfectly all the time. The point is that spouses in bad marriages, who have low self-esteem, have usually been dishonored more consistently than people in healthier marriages. Sometimes this happens because people get busy…there seems to be less time to communicate properly, spend time together, or nurture each other as a husband and wife or friends would do. Many female clients complain their husband "never pays attention to me", or "never spends time with me". I hear men say, "my wife treats me like an ATM", or "she cares more about being a mother than being a wife".

Notice how these complaints are all about actions, not about the words used by their spouse. That is a key point to remember about honoring each other in marriage. Honor is most clearly displayed and paid when our behavior reflects a high reverence for the person we hold in high regard. Without such action, honor is incomplete, it is lip service. Honor is an internal attitude of respect, courtesy and reverence, but it requires an appropriate outward expression to convey this attitude.

When people don't honor that which honors them, they decay from within. This is what happens when you begin to lose self-respect and self-esteem – you stop honoring yourself because there's less and less within to honor. You lose your own voice and your own sense of worthwhileness and your meaning and purpose as a person beyond your role as a spouse. You begin to decay from within.

Honoring one's dignity in a troubled marriage is difficult, but it's particularly difficult when there's a disconnect between one spouse wanting to recover self-esteem and dignity, and the other one at odds with what that requires. There are lots of ways to honor your dignity in a bad marriage, but it's particularly challenging when your spouse intentionally blocks you from doing so, or makes things so intolerable when you do, that sustaining your efforts long-term is impossible.

I know this is true because of my experience with my wife. One of our rules is to never fight or humiliate each other in public. We are committed to "honoring" each other publicly, and stay mindful of the things which we each would perceive as embarrassing or provocative to diminish the likelihood of public dishonoring. We simply believe that fighting and causing a spectacle doesn't honor us individually or as a couple. Instead, if something happens to upset one of us, we wait until we get home and then discuss it. That can be hard to do if your spouse has really irritated you, but it is possible.

Anyway, in my marriage, I learned very quickly that dishonoring her by showing a lack of respect or regard for her dignity and personal integrity would lead me back to divorce court for a third time.

When I listened to her interpretation of what happened, I understood that from her perspective, what I did made her feel dishonored – I'd belittled her, ridiculed her, and disparaged her. While I didn't understand the significance of this lesson or grasp the totality of it for many years, my wife's influence and vigil on both of our self-esteems has illustrated that when you don't honor yourself properly, you can't honor the marriage properly. In other words, if you don't hold yourself in a high regard, then how can you hold your marriage in a high regard? The reality is that my wife's self-esteem was intact so she was able to stand up for herself and admonish me for dishonoring her, embarrassing her, and disregarding her dignity and integrity. Without knowing her value, she wouldn't have thought to speak up and stop me from ever dishonoring her again.

The journey I outline in this book seeks to honor you and your dignity by helping you figure out what that seed is, and build a life which honors or dignifies it. The journey, either in knowing what a healthy and respectful relationship entails, working to save your marriage, or maximizing all the opportunities of divorce, is designed to help you sort out what people, places, things, habits, careers, past traumas, unresolved pain, etc..., are contributing to your low self-worth, and find out ways to get rid of them, or deal with them and thrive in dignity and healthy self-worth anyway.

That is why dignity and understanding, and what it REALLY means, is the best gift I can help you give yourself. You will feel SO MUCH BETTER about yourself just by reading this book because you'll learn where your negative thoughts about yourself come from, and clearly see how to distinguish truth from lies about who you are and what you're worth.

People who lack integrity say one thing and then do the other – there are parts or pieces to them which aren't always obvious because their words or actions conceal them.

You need to figure out if your intended soulmate or spouse will tolerate your full expression of who you are within the marriage. Can that special person entertain your evolution as a person of integrity and a person who stands on conviction and is a whole person – the sum of all their parts?

I once represented a man who lived with a totally dictatorial wife and had stopped thinking for himself years before coming to me for divorce advice. He shared that any time he attempted to speak his own mind or express an opinion about anything important to him or their children, his wife absolutely refused to allow it. She shut him down immediately or pretended she didn't hear him.

He said, "I tried to save the marriage but it was impossible because she couldn't tolerate the real me. For 12 years, I let her mold me into the man she wanted me to be and I went along with it. It wasn't until I heard you talking about integrity and self-worth that I realized just how much of myself I shut down or 'splintered off' just to appease her and keep our marriage intact."

"Pacifying her for all those years cost me a lot, and the heaviest toll on my self-worth was feeling powerless in my own marriage because I didn't have the power to be my own person. Rather than asserting myself and risking an argument, I let her control the outcome of everything, which gave her all the power. Jack, when I tried to apply your advice to save the marriage, she didn't want to see the opinionated, articulate person I was in the rest of the areas of my life – I could only be 'that guy' at the office – at home she had to be the boss. When I realized she deliberately shut me down for her own selfish gains, and she was unwilling to renegotiate or reconsider how to rebuild the marriage, I packed my bags and left. Just because my dignity was a non-issue for her, didn't mean it would be a non-issue for me anymore."

Rebuilding anything requires work – there are no easy buttons to push. Rebuild means you acknowledge that something is broken or nearly broken, and there are pieces to put back together. It's difficult to actually look at the shattered pieces of your life and of yourself. Sometimes you see things you don't want to see, or didn't know were there and broken. Initially, you feel shocked and then you might be angry and vengeful at your spouse if you believe he or she is to blame for the brokenness.

If this resentment builds up and you're still married, it might be exceptionally difficult to overcome those feelings and deal with them, when you're stuck looking at this person over the breakfast table every morning – especially when that person isn't receptive to your growth, and resents the changes in the relationship. But you must press through and try to forgive. You can rebuild what's broken in an entirely new way than what was there originally. The script can be rewritten. The pieces might be the same but how they fit together can be fresh. And you might discover that the cause of their breakage isn't at all what you thought it was.

For now, as you struggle to determine if your self-esteem can be rebuilt within the marriage, I'll offer the most basic definition – self-esteem is your thoughts about yourself. Either you think of yourself in a positive way or a negative way.

Self-esteem can't be rebuilt overnight, especially when you are trying to do so in an unhappy, yet hopefully not unsalvageable marriage. And sometimes self-esteem can't be recovered in marriage if your spouse has a vested interest in your low self-worth, i.e. they abuse you, have narcissistic tendencies, etc. But there's something important to remember while you contemplate divorce – the first step you need to take right now is exercising self-compassion.

Having some compassion for yourself right now, right where you are is important because you need to understand that all the issues and problems in your marriage and in your "inner self life" are not all your fault. You have survived circumstances and people and experiences which have hurt you and affected your life, choice of spouse, etc......in more ways than you are aware right now. Our tendency is to blame ourselves and criticize ourselves because we think it's "our fault", or that something intrinsic about ourselves caused the problems in the marriage.

Self-flagellation is common when we feel badly about ourselves, or our spouse daily says or does things to reinforce our negative thoughts. But compassion produces far greater results than criticism and blame, and my mission is to do all I can to help you secure far greater results in all areas of your life than you can imagine. You've already demonstrated tremendous courage if you've accepted my message and are willing to embark on the journey of rebuilding your self-worth, so even if you think you are the most worthless, vile, evil, and ugly monster on earth right now, I know you have the courage to try giving yourself a break.

Chapter 3

Before Telling Your Spouse You Want a Divorce

Think Like a Business Person
Legally dissolving your marriage is essentially a business transaction. In many ways, your lawyer is your business advisor, and needs you to provide essential information about your assets, liabilities and net worth. Gathering necessary information before telling your spouse you want a divorce will accomplish three important things:

- Your actions affirm your decision. By acting like a person getting divorced, you are less likely to experience ambivalence.

- You alleviate the need to retrieve the information later when your spouse might not be willing to let you access it, or has hidden it away. If you can get what you need before your spouse has a chance to act, you are more likely to get a better handle on the full picture of your marital assets and liabilities.

- The earlier you and your attorney can evaluate pertinent information, the better you can develop realistic goals and an effective strategy for success.

Before your divorce meeting, make copies and gather important documents and items that will be necessary in your divorce proceedings. This includes, but is not limited to, birth certificates, marriage licenses, passports, Social

Security cards, bank statements, safe deposit keys, stock certificates, insurance information, mortgage documents, property deeds, will and trust documents, operating licenses, business incorporation certificates, retirement plans, etc. Gather these important materials and keep them in a safe place that your spouse cannot access.

You want to approach the business side of the divorce like a business person – good business people are always prepared, and think a few steps ahead. They act with integrity, and don't intentionally harm their adversary.

An easy way to think about this is to imagine if you never had access to anything in your files again after the divorce meeting. What do you need for your life to proceed smoothly, and what do you need copies of for the "just in case" moments? What does your spouse need for his or her life to proceed smoothly? I'm not advising you to steal your spouse's passport, Social Security card, or other documents having nothing to do with you or the marriage. Leave those things behind, but be sure to make copies. Don't take things out of spite. Vindictiveness will get you nowhere.

A Sticky Issue

Once the client is certain he or she wants to file for a divorce, I ask if there is anything the spouse could use to embarrass, humiliate, blackmail, or hurt the situation, either presently or in the future. I'm referring to tangible items such as sex tapes, inappropriate photographs, letters, criminal material, etc. It's also important to consider any inappropriate material posted online, or texts and photographs stored in your cell phone or your spouse's.

Several years ago, in Charlotte County Florida, I represented a husband who was furious over his wife's custody requests. He asserted she was an unfit mother and told me he could prove it. One afternoon he showed up and produced the "evidence." It was a photograph of his wife engaged in oral sex with another man. The photo was taken in front of a fireplace and I could see Christmas stockings hanging from the mantel. The stockings had the names of my client, his wife, and all the children – clearly this act occurred in the marital home. As he held the photograph before me, it was obvious that he thought he'd produced the smoking gun, I asked, "Who took the picture? Cecil B. De Mille?"

"I did," he responded flatly.

"If this were entered into evidence, the judge would think far less of you than your wife."

One Caveat

My suggestions imply that you act with discretion. If you don't think you can accomplish these tasks without alerting your spouse, it's perfectly acceptable to skip this advice.

The discovery stage of the divorce process enables your attorney to subpoena these records and access the important information. This advice is for those who can access some or all of the files privately, make copies on a home printer/copier, or travel to a copier, and return them as found.

Hannah

Early in my career, I represented Hannah, a young woman from New York. I was never able to determine whether Hannah was a drug addict or an alcoholic, but she always arrived at my office under the influence of something. I cared about Hannah and worried about her obvious substance addiction.

One morning I called Hannah and asked her to bring her mother to our next meeting. Even with her mother, Hannah showed up intoxicated. I didn't waste time getting to the reason behind my invitation to mom. I confronted her about Hannah.

"Your daughter is either a drug addict or an alcoholic. You must help her get clean."

Mom was outraged. She couldn't speak at first. She just kept gasping for air and looking around the room – everywhere except in Hannah's direction. She seemed to be shocked I would speak to her directly.

"Mom, I've been representing Hannah in her divorce for months, and I've never seen her sober. Your daughter is sick, and she needs you right now!"

"Mr. Long, how dare you have me come to your office only to make such vicious, false accusations!?" She was furious.

"Look at her! She's on something. You must accept the truth and intervene." Hannah didn't say a word.

Her mother continued to carry on with her indignant denials and didn't even notice Hannah's silence, or glance at her. She grabbed Hannah and walked out my door in a huff.

My phone rang weeks later. Hannah was dead. Hannah had been found in her home, unconscious and lying in a pool of blood. She died of a gunshot wound. The newspaper reported it was suicide.

This case confirmed that nothing is worth keeping my mouth shut and hiding the truth from clients. My direct style was shocking, and maybe next time it would shock someone into action before it's too late. My phone rang.....three years later.....a homicide.

Murder in the Family

"Mr. Long?"

"Yes?" I grumbled groggily into the mouthpiece of my bedroom phone.

"This is Junior – My father's dead." "Of natural causes?" I asked. "'Fraid not."

My eyes shot open. I looked at the clock. It was 4:54 in the morning. "Oh my God. I'm on my way."

I leapt out of bed and showered at lightning pace. I hurriedly dressed, grabbed my briefcase and flew out the door. As I got into my car, I shouted back to cancel my appointments and court appearances that day because I was headed upstate to Maple Leaf Farm.

As I drove up the interstate toward the Hudson Valley, I was still struggling to make sense of that early morning phone call. Al Sr. was embroiled in a heated and terribly nasty divorce battle with his soon-to-be ex, Mary, whom I represented. During their 44 years together, they had raised their children on the family-owned and operated apple farm in the Hudson Valley. The marriage ended after both parties had become so full of resentment and anger due to the stress of being married and business partners, that they couldn't stand the sight of each other any longer.

At that time in New York, no-fault divorce did not exist. One party had to prove the other was to blame for the marital demise. But neither partner wanted to be the "fall guy", and there was no readily-available or obvious reason why the marriage was no longer working. Infidelity wasn't an issue, but abuse was. Both Mary and Al Sr. were just so stubborn, and they had strong work ethics and values. The marriage had failed and was irretrievably broken. (It's a perfect example of why no-fault laws are such a positive aspect of the modernization of divorce law during my lifetime. Blame and fault are irrelevant in the eyes of the law today, allowing couples to simply focus on the present and future rather than forcing them to re-hash the skeletons from the past and demonize each other for marital mistakes.)

Eventually Al Sr. accused Mary of having an addiction to alcohol and pills, and attempted to use that as the grounds for divorce. It was outrageous and Mary was shocked. She drank moderately socially, and took prescription medication only to control her blood pressure issues. But the real problem in the divorce was determining how to deal with the family farm. Neither one was willing to split it, sell it, or let it go. They each were hell-bent on keeping it all to themselves. The farm was a gorgeous property with a commercially valuable apple orchard stretching for countless acres. And in the middle of it all sat a spectacular seven-bedroom, brick farmhouse.

When I turned off the country road and onto the long driveway toward the house, an eerie uneasiness washed over me. I parked next to a few police cruisers left haphazardly in the driveway. The front door was wide open.

I found Mary and the children seated around a large kitchen table drinking coffee and saying very little. I felt their eyes follow me as I approached their mother's chair. I leaned down and whispered, "How're ya doing, Mary?"

She looked up at me casually and said, "Never better."

I was dumbfounded. I certainly didn't expect a response like that, especially when I could tell from the look in her eye that she really meant it.

Still unsure of what had happened exactly, I made nervous small talk with the family until the medical examiner signaled that they were wrapping things up.

I learned that just before dawn, the husband had gone into Mary's bedroom to take a picture of her asleep next to the nightstand which happened to be covered in pill bottles and an empty bottle or two of vodka. The camera flash, along with the sound of the creaking bedroom door had apparently awakened Mary and frightened her. She thought Al Sr. was an intruder, so she grabbed the shotgun she kept under the bed and fired at the shadowy figure she saw lurking near the door. As she blasted away, the force of the impact knocked him back out the door to his death.

I didn't know what to make of this story at first. I knew they were battling over the property, and neither one had any overly compelling argument for how it should be awarded. I also knew they were both increasingly angry and bitter and these negative emotions fed their absolute determination to keep the farm. Al Sr.'s argument that he should get the property because it would surely fall into misuse, disrepair, and financial disaster under the auspices of "Mary the Drunk", had never gained traction because he couldn't present any corroborating evidence. Was this his attempt to prove his story, by taking pictures of her passed out next to her booze and pills?

Obviously, this was not the way I wanted to "win" the case. This was a nightmare. And it scared me. Mary's case is an extreme example of how greed, lust for money, years of resentment, and vindictiveness can collide in a divorce. The bitterness in the hearts of Mary and Al Sr. had become so poisonous that they'd become unable to think rationally or behave appropriately.

Plan Escape

It's important to make arrangements for where to go after your divorce meeting in case things get ugly. Where will you go? Where will your children go? What about your pets? It's important to pack a bag in advance, and secure a place to stay. Even if you don't end up following through on the plan, you cannot underestimate your spouse. You have no way of knowing how the divorce meeting will turn out, or how your spouse will react. The only way to protect yourself is to plan for the worst and have a safe place to go if necessary.

I recommend staying with a trusted friend or relative. I think it's best to go anywhere you can find loyal, encouraging support from people who love and care about you. Some people want to be alone, and go to a hotel which is fine too. Consider what will be best for you physically and emotionally – everyone is different. If you have children, they should be somewhere safe during your divorce meeting. Your children should not be present when you tell your spouse the marriage is over. There should be no chance that they arrive in the middle of the meeting either. There is no place for children anywhere in the divorce meeting.

But, what does all this have to do with self-esteem?

Don't allow low self-esteem to prevent you from taking advantage of the important opportunity of planning for a successful divorce. You must begin to act for yourself. Taking responsibility for yourself and your future can begin by taking control of how you can help yourself in the early stages of the divorce. Also, a plan alleviates the stress of the situation because you are prepared for contingencies, and when you take control it boosts your confidence. It can really help the divorce process progress smoothly when you start it off right – preparing and behaving civilly is both dignified, and promotes healthy self-esteem.

Your actions speak for you – which will you choose?

Option One: **Plan and execute.** This option requires that you take responsibility for the divorce in advance by carefully planning how to extricate yourself from the marriage. Prepare your documents, investigate your options with an attorney, and have a mature divorce meeting with your spouse. Plan how, when and what to say to your spouse to officially end the marriage and execute it. You might think of the divorce meeting as reaching the peak of an enormous mountain. How will you get there? Are your supplies adequate? Did you plan for contingencies?

Option Two: **Wing it.** This option throws caution to the wind and doesn't hold you accountable at all. You "wing" the discussion with your spouse, not taking time to plan what to say or how. You have nowhere to go and no plan to fall back on if your spouse kicks you out. You have no bag of clothes and important documents if the locks have been changed. Again, if the divorce meeting is like a mountain, how are you expecting a successful climb to the top when you failed to chart the best course, you wore sandals instead of boots, and you ran out of water in the first three hours?

A sign of healthy self-esteem is when you can honestly evaluate your situation, consider what's in your best interest, and develop a strategy to overcome and succeed. People with low self-esteem cannot bear to hold themselves accountable for what happens to them in the next five minutes, let alone the next five weeks or five months. They take one look at the mountain and run the other way. But once you've hit your misery threshold and there's no acceptable alternative to divorce, the mountain is there whether you like it or not. This is your moment to start over. Just because you've run from every other mountain in your past doesn't mean you have to run from this one too.

Use this as a fresh start and plan your expedition.

It is much easier to plan, than it is to pick up the pieces when winging it results in disaster. Clients who want to divorce smart, divorce with dignity, and recover their self- esteem, choose option one – the only option if you want a divorce done right.

Divorce styles and strategies reveal a lot about a couple and the individuals themselves. Self-esteem can directly impact your net gain in the divorce. If you don't take control over your divorce, someone else will – and you might get royally screwed. One person can completely dominate and dictate nearly every aspect of a divorce when his or her spouse has not a shred of self-esteem, and can't take responsibility.

Ted / Paula

Ted had been married to Paula for several years and they never had any children. He told me that he'd just asked her for a divorce and though upset, Paula was compliant and calm. Their marriage was over, he said, because they simply "drifted apart".

Ted's main concern was money. Paula hadn't worked during their marriage and their marital assets totaled more than $11 million. Like most men, Ted feared that Paula would hire an aggressive attorney who would motivate Paula to request large alimony payments and take half of the marital estate. He wanted to know what he could do to prevent this.

It wasn't hard to surmise that Ted was a controlling husband, and controlling husbands typically have wives with little or no self-esteem. Such wives are used to being controlled (even when they can't admit it to themselves), and when confronted with divorce, most of them are paralyzed, unable to act in their own best interest.

I explained to Ted that mediation is the best way to go if you want to avoid hefty attorney's fees, and maintain civility. I informed Ted of his worst-case scenario – losing millions and then possibly having to pay alimony.

Several weeks later, Ted invited me to lunch at one of the ritziest restaurants in town. He wanted to thank me for the "good advice" and tell me what happened with Paula.

"We went to a mediator as you recommended, Jack. I'm so glad we didn't involve attorneys, and Paula agreed to work it out ourselves. It saved me expensive legal fees!"

He smiled and thanked me for "elevating his needs above my own"! Integrity.

Paula is a perfect example of what can happen if you don't open your eyes to the possibilities of divorce. Not only did Paula have the money to hire an attorney, but she had the opportunity to ask questions or look for records of their net worth and assets. Don't let your lack of self-esteem suffocate you like Paula's did. Don't be a Paula.

How to Tell Your Spouse You Want a Divorce

There are right and wrong ways to tell your spouse you want a divorce. The easiest way to determine if your plan is right or wrong is to ask yourself the following question: ***"Is this how I would like my spouse to tell me?"***

I'm always willing to instruct my clients, or provide the appropriate script, about how to do this in order to minimize ugliness, miscommunication and quite frankly, combat.

Something to keep in mind when planning the divorce conversation, or divorce meeting, is that it will comprise the final moments of your marriage. Although your marriage is not officially dissolved until the judge signs the decree, I believe the final moments of your marriage occur in this private act – it's the moment where the disengagement begins. How do you want these final moments to go? Which character do you want to be in that moment? How do you want to remember the final acts of the marriage? You probably don't want it to end in a heated frenzy of cursing, accusations, name-calling and rage. Surely you've both had enough of those scenes, right?

Once you've made the irreversible decision to end your marriage, there's no possible apology from your spouse that will make any difference. There's no need to fight, no need to reconsider, and no need to do anything but behave like the mature adult you need to be. It's time to tend to the business of dissolving what has long been dead.

What Are the Right Words to Use in Telling My Spouse I Want a Divorce?

The best way to tell your spouse you want a divorce is to sit down and calmly say, "I've made the irreversible decision to put our dead marriage to sleep."

My client, June, practiced reciting the sentence for days. She would say it aloud in the mirror until it came out gently, calmly, and effectively. When she finally delivered it to her husband at the divorce meeting, it went exactly as she hoped. To her surprise, her husband was the one who became overwhelmed with grief, but he didn't try to negotiate or change her mind. Since she was not awash in sobs and tears, he could clearly see that she meant business. June allowed him time to feel the grief, and empathized with his pain without giving into it. Within an hour, he agreed.

June made her plan, stuck to her script and felt very pleased with how things went at the divorce meeting. That victory was significant in her journey to recapture self-esteem. She experienced the wonderful results of taking responsibility and began to believe in herself for the first time in six years. It was a major accomplishment and it set the tone for how she proceeded throughout the rest of her divorce.

The Divorce Meeting: Actually Delivering the Words

You have no control over how your spouse responds and reacts at the divorce meeting. But you do have control over the words you select, the timing of your delivery, and how you choose to react to his or her reaction. Refuse to engage in negotiations or fight. Persist in your resolve that you will only do this once – you don't want to have this conversation over and over again, so make this one shot count.

Telling your spouse you want a divorce in the proper manner is also important because it has the potential to impact the emotional pitch of the entire divorce process. Witnessing your spouse's reaction to your words can provide clues for you and your attorney as to what kind of emotions will dictate your spouse's behavior during the divorce. Look for anything that can enlighten you regarding your spouse's motives or goals for a settlement. If you can stick to your script and maintain a calm, peaceful demeanor, you will be in a better position to gauge where your spouse is emotionally. When you aren't hysterically emotional during the divorce meeting, your spouse can respond to the issue of divorce, not your hysterics.

During the divorce meeting, tell your spouse where your children are, unless you have reason to believe he or she might harm them or become angry about it. You don't want to arouse suspicion that you're using the kids as weapons to hurt your spouse. The divorce meeting is an important step in setting the tone for how you will co-parent so honor your spouse as a parent and put the best interests of your children first. **It is totally unacceptable to ever use your children as pawns** so don't start now.

In a Perfect Divorce Meeting

In a perfect world, you will both agree that the dead marriage should be put to sleep, and commit to treating each other as amicably as possible throughout the divorce process. The ideal conversation would go as follows: first, you state your sentence calmly and directly. Don't make any apologies for your decision or say anything like "I'm sorry but I just can't do this anymore." This could be perceived as an accusation or blame, since "not being able to do something anymore" is a decision based on emotion. You are keeping as much emotion as you can out of it.

Second, allow your spouse time to absorb what you said and respond honestly. There's no need to rush or say anything else. Always remember that all you control is *your* words, *your* tone, and *your* decision.

In a perfect world, there will be no fight. Deep down, most spouses in dead marriages know it should end, and will be grateful to finally conclude the "should we or shouldn't we" debate. This doesn't mean the decision has been fully absorbed and accepted immediately, but it's not uncommon for both the "dumper" and the "dumpee" to share equally in the sense of relief that a decision has been made. Being in limbo and uncertain about the future of your marriage is terribly stressful and it helps when you can each at least appreciate that this part is over.

After your spouse is resigned to the finality of the decision, and neither of you is overwhelmed by emotions, you both might wonder what to do next. Some couples begin making plans. Please proceed with caution if this happens. It's important to avoid making promises or firm statements as to what you want in the divorce, or what you're willing to give up. However, if your spouse is willing to make these overtures, pay attention. This is useful information that your attorney can use in developing a strategy for your case. If your spouse promises you anything, acknowledge the offer by repeating it back like this, "Thank you for offering to pay my health insurance for three years. I really appreciate that. I know we have a lot to figure out and I hope we can keep a positive attitude and work together during this process." Take mental note of what is offered, requested, or demanded, and tell your attorney.

If your spouse asks when to get a lawyer or tell others that a decision to divorce has been reached, I advise waiting a few days until you can both settle in to the reality of the decision. There's no need to run out and tell the whole world of your new marital status until you can better wrap your head around things. Of course, the smart spouse, you, already have an attorney standing by if your spouse goes crazy during this period and files immediately. But if you can show that you're non-adversarial, calm and collected, it won't incite your spouse to go on the defensive right away.

End the conversation by affirming that you're both doing the right thing. I suggest telling your spouse you're committed to getting through the last act of your marriage with dignity and civility. Just make sure you have a plan for where to go in case you need to separate for an evening or a little while. Use your best judgment about whether to stay or go.

In a Not-So-Perfect Divorce Meeting

Believe it or not, the "perfect world scenario" happens more than people think. I believe this is because both spouses have finally run out of the desire to keep fighting. They are tired. But in many other cases, spouses are energized by their anger, frustration and resentment, and the divorce meeting is far from ideal. It usually begins to unravel when the dumper, you, lets the conversation escalate and become a back-and-forth, tit-for-tat, battle royale. When you allow your spouse to bargain, or threaten you with retaliations, such as wiping out the bank accounts, taking the kids, etc., fear and anger have displaced peace and acceptance.

This retaliatory technique is a threat itself, geared to scare you into changing your mind. It does not indicate acceptance but rather inhibits your spouse from dealing with the reality of your decision. When we latch on to anger and outbursts, it is likely out of denial, fear, and loss of control. This is why you must remain calm, leave at the first hint of ugliness, anger or threats, and have an exit strategy in place.

The goal is to find a way to have the divorce meeting that will foster recovery of both spouses, promote the dignity of both, and minimize harm to children.

Isabelle

One client who did not understand my message that litigation, in most cases, benefits the lawyer and not the client was Isabelle. She and her soon-to-be-ex-husband argued about everything and spent almost two years negotiating their settlement.

Her bitterness sucked all the life out of her and all that was left was a middle-aged, well-dressed woman with fake boobs and big hair. Anyway, after months of haggling over every piece of property they owned, we were on the brink of trial.

Isabelle and I met her soon-to-be ex and his lawyer at the courthouse for one last round of attempted negotiations. As usual, the negotiations were going nowhere and we were at a stalemate. I suggested a break and took Isabelle outside for a chat hoping the fresh air might do us both some good. Outside the courthouse I decided to try one last time to convince Isabelle to give her husband "go away money". I explained she'd save more by paying him $25,000 today instead of dragging out the case and forcing it to trial.

I'm not easily intimidated, but Isabelle was so bitter and vindictive, and had become a very menacing figure in her fury. It didn't help that she was wearing five-inch stiletto heels either. As I tried to make my case one last time, Isabelle towered over me with a scowl, her low-cut leopard blouse and cleavage was right in my face. In fact, when we were nose to nose, my face was in it, and when we were toes to toes, my nose was in it! I could hear her tapping the pavement. I was surprised she was letting me finish without interruption, so I took the opportunity to explain my reasoning. When done, I looked up and awaited her response.

Isabelle grabbed me by my tie and said, "I wouldn't give that man the spit off a dog's____!" With that, she released me and marched back inside the courthouse. Wow! I had never heard that expression in all my years of handling divorce clients, and thankfully I never heard it again!

Some months later, everything I warned would happen, happened. Isabelle lost far more than if had she had been able to negotiate.

Chapter 4

Divorce Law and Lawyers

Divorcing with dignity really can be the best way to either avoid or minimize bitterness. It's hard to let that anger go if you've been resentful for so many years, but it's the only way you can look back on this period in your life and recognize that you handled your divorce the right way. That is the most precious gift of divorce done right and with dignity. Harboring resentment, jealousy, envy or hate will prevent you from seeing all you have gained.

Victim Exploitation
When clients don't know how to be anything but a victim, they look for an attorney who will indulge them in their "victimhood", and take responsibility for the entire divorce process.....or that kind of attorney finds them.

Self-esteem is not restored overnight, and when the marriage ends and they want to start exercising some control, they often look for an unnecessarily aggressive attorney to do the dirty work for them. Hiring aggressive attorneys gives them a sense of power but in reality, they want the "junkyard dogs" to bark and bite because they aren't strong enough to fight themselves. Exploited spouses want to show their exes they can no longer be manipulated and use a surrogate, the aggressive attorney, to communicate that message. It gives them a false sense of power and accomplishment to send the Rottweiler in to attack the spouse, demand huge support payments and anything else they can get their hands on.

They want revenge – they want their spouse to pay. They want to hurt their ex like they were hurt. So they look for Rottweilers to represent them.

Victimized, exploited spouses with low self-esteem feel they can't fight for themselves. It drives them to use the courts to stand up to controlling spouses for the first time in years. They need attorneys to do this for them, and there are far too many willing to do so. If you know you have self-esteem issues heading into a divorce, and you don't want to sacrifice what little is left, look for an attorney who will help you rebuild what you've lost, who will work with you and encourage you to develop your goals for the divorce, assert your needs, and who will treat you with respect and dignity.

Conversely, the underlying reason I've fired clients is because *I can only help those who are willing to help themselves.* Even clients who aren't receptive to my self-esteem message, and are only dealing with the clinical aspects of divorce, must be prepared and willing to help their attorney with their case.

It helps if they're sober too. One memorable client that I fired was Tammy. Tammy barely got five appointments out of me until I cut her loose. She showed up to every appointment with two things: a blood-alcohol level of at least 0.12 and a random boyfriend. Tammy's appointments were never later than 10:30 a.m., and she would stumble through the oversized lobby doors of my office, hanging onto the arm of Mr. "We Just Met Last Night".

One morning she showed up late again. My office door was open and I heard her enter the building. She was giggling with her boyfriend-of-the-day, and apologized for being late as my secretary tried to offer her a cup of coffee. She declined. "No thanks, I'm not all that thirsty. We finished our Jack and Cokes in the parking lot."

That did it. I jumped out of my chair and marched out to the lobby. I said, "Tammy, for all I care Jack Daniels can be your new divorce attorney!" I simply can't sit by and watch people ignore my advice and continue to engage in self-destructive behavior.

What If I Keep Firing My Lawyers?

Typically, that's an indication that the problems lie with you, not your former attorneys. There are many reasons why clients terminate a representation, but if it keeps happening, it is likely that all the attorneys are saying the same thing – and the client doesn't want to hear it.

So, they lawyer shop. They go around looking for an attorney who will tell them what they want to hear, or make them feel like they are more willing to do what it takes to provide the result they want.

Melissa

Ten years ago, I represented Melissa, a bright, warm, accomplished accountant. She hired me after a failed mediation attempt with her previous attorney, a woman I didn't know who practiced near Tampa. Melissa explained that during the mediation, they'd reached an agreement on child custody but the meeting collapsed when the mediator mentioned the word "alimony". As the breadwinner, Melissa was apt to lose a substantial portion of her net worth to her parasitic husband, Kevin. Kevin was 52, athletic, tan, and was a "stay-at-home dad".

I quickly discovered that there was nothing "stay-at-home" about Kevin. He was one spoiled SOB. The daily sum total of his homemaking was three hours. As an accountant, Melissa would leave for the office early in the morning, so Kevin would get the children up, fed, and ready for school. His last task of the day was dropping them at the bus stop at 8:30 am.

Rather than returning home to tend to typical household duties, Kevin took full advantage of the lifestyle Melissa provided. He'd spend his days on the golf course, or fishing, or using the gym at the country club and treating himself to post-workout massages. Kevin hired a maid to do his work. She did the laundry, cleaning, shopping, and cooking.

By mid-afternoon, appointments were over and Melissa would pick up the kids, run to soccer practices and ballet, fix dinner, help with homework, get them showered, and then collapse so she could get up before dawn. She never saw Kevin – he was too busy out partying, going to clubs, indulging in lavish dinners, and living like a spoiled brat. I suspected he had a girlfriend or five on the side, but Melissa didn't suspect anything, and he never confessed.

After years of marriage, Melissa couldn't stand it, and asked the bloodsucking parasite for a divorce. Kevin, as expected, was furious. It meant the end of his cushy lifestyle, and he came after the money. The good news was that they agreed to a fair joint child custody arrangement so that left money as the primary issue to resolve.

Melissa explained, "There we were, all four of us, in the middle of the mediation session when the mediator turned to me and said, 'Monthly alimony to Kevin in the amount of $15,000.' Jack, I thought I was going to fall out of my chair. Alimony was almost never mentioned. I remember my lawyer bringing it up during our first meeting, but she told me not to worry because it wouldn't be very much. We never discussed it again."

"I was so angry and shocked I could barely speak. I just grabbed my purse, slammed the door, and never went back!"

I was surprised to hear the lawyer had barely mentioned alimony. Whether it's accurate or not, I don't know. I wasn't there during all their meetings. What matters is Melissa's perception that she had been set up with unrealistic expectations. She believed the lawyer had overpromised thinking it

would help secure Melissa as a client. By the time Melissa came to see me, she was still reeling from the alimony disaster at the mediation, as well as the emotional anguish from the divorce itself.

In the end, we went back to mediation and resolved the case. I negotiated alimony to a more palatable figure, and Melissa was okay with that. She was relieved to get away from her freeloading husband, and thanked me for helping to restore her self-esteem so she could be a better role model for her children.

Chapter 5

Bad Behavior and the Indignity of Abuse

The Consequences of Abuse
One of the results of being in my business for so long is that you get to know the patterns of abusive spouses. Thousands of abuse victims have come through my office describing terrible abusive marriages and during the latter part of my career, many of them have been shocked that I'm able to describe their soon-to-be ex's tirades or behavior nearly exactly without ever having met them. The consequences of abuse affect self-worth, decision-making, and lifestyle choices.

One of the most shocking things I've witnessed throughout my career is abuse victims who don't even know they've been abused! I'm alarmed by the hidden epidemic of verbal or emotional abuse. There are many reasons why smart, educated, worldly, and otherwise sophisticated people cannot identify their spouse as an abuser. Sometimes this happens because they were raised in an abusive home, and simply don't know any other way a spouse should treat the other partner in a marriage. Witnessing abuse as a child conditions them to believe abuse is "normal", and blinds them to the abuse perpetrated upon them as adults.

One memorable client, Anna, was extremely successful and held two advanced degrees from top tier schools. She was raised in a non-abusive home by two psychologists who specialized in treating victims of abuse, and never recognized that her husband was horribly verbally and emotionally abusive.

After a few months of marriage counseling and private therapy, Anna came to see me.

Anna

"Jack, I almost fell off my chair when the psychiatrist questioned why I'd tolerated such obvious verbal and emotional abuse. I knew my husband was a big jerk and I didn't deserve all his screaming and viciousness, but it never crossed my mind that it was 'abuse'. I thought abuse meant physical or sexual abuse, and it was always obvious if you were a victim. It never occurred to me his screaming, name-calling, and insistence my feelings were irrelevant was abuse. I guess I always thought he was behaving that way because of stress at work, or because I should've known better than to leave the cap off the toothpaste again."

Many abused spouses spend a lot of time and energy making excuses or justifying their abuser's behavior. They find reasons to explain why something they'd done had resulted in an abusive outburst. Instead of directing the blame and shame where it belongs – on the abuser – victims frequently excuse the abuse by blaming circumstances, stress and worst of all, themselves. But there is never any excuse for any kind of abuse and there is nobody to blame for the abuse but the abuser.

The Self-Fulfilling Cycle of Abuse and Low Self-Worth

Abusers are excellent at blaming everyone but themselves for their atrocious behavior, and after years of demolishing or damaging their victims' self-esteem, it's easy for the victim to find fault within. Abuse damages our self-esteem and the more we suffer from low self-esteem, the more we tend to make excuses, misdirect blame, etc. This is a hallmark of abuse. Without healthy self-esteem, abuse victims often lack the confidence and courage to leave the marriage, and the self-fulfilling cycle of abuse continues. They continue to be victims, but they are not the only victims.

Children of Abuse
A child in an abusive home pays the ultimate price. The nature of abusive homes saps all who dwell there of healthy self-respect and dignity. This means victims and witnesses suffer the consequences of abuse. Witnessing abuse is just as dangerous as being abused yourself, particularly when it happens over and over. Children who witness a parent being abused develop lots of intense anger because they feel powerless to stop the abuse.

The other problem with raising children in an abusive home is that they are not provided with an example or role model of a functional adult with healthy self-worth. They are set up for a life of low self-worth and many later abuse or become victims of abuse in subsequent relationships. The cycle of abuse almost always continues and it will be your legacy to them, or part of it if you don't take action now.

The Abusers Themselves

Lots of abused spouses tell me they tolerated the abuse for many years because of various reasons, but many are shocked to hear me say tolerating that abuse was not only a disservice to themselves, but also to their abuser. Abuse hurts the dignity of the abuser because it reinforces the abuser's low self-respect.

Abusing others is about acting out their own feelings of unworthiness, guilt or pain, and mistreating others as a misguided way to assert their power, or self-determination. But abuse actually is a sign of little power, and abusing others by words or behavior only leads them further and further away from their own dignity seeds.

Getting Out

Recognizing and acknowledging abuse as "abuse" is one thing – deciding what to do about the abuse is another.

Claire was certainly headed for a life of misery and victimization when she first walked in to my office for her consultation. Without a shred of self-esteem left, she was the poster child for the "doormat spouse" who tolerates any and all mistreatment and abuse perpetrated upon her by an abusive spouse. Years after her divorce was finalized, she arrived unexpectedly at my office. My secretary announced that a special visitor had arrived and when I walked into the lobby to greet my guest, I almost didn't recognize her.

Claire looked COMPLETELY different from when I'd last seen her. She waltzed into my office after returning from St. Maarten. Claire radiated confidence and happiness and I was dazzled by her tanned skin and broad smile as we chatted. Our conversation was memorable because she'd made a 180-degree turn in her appearance, attitude, and mood since her divorce, and according to her, it was all because she was *"set free to discover her self-worth after divorcing an emotional abuser."*

Claire

"It was like I was seeing a ray of sunlight for the first time in long time. As soon as I realized he'd been abusing me and it was his abusive nature, rather than my forgetfulness or clumsiness which caused his awful behavior, I could stop believing I was a bad person who deserved the fate I'd suffered."

"It was as if I was finally free to dare myself to dream what my life could be like if I believed, if only for a moment, that I was a woman worthy and deserving of even a small fraction more respect than I'd been getting. With the assistance of self-help books and some more therapy, I learned he was in a prison of abusive tendencies and behavior, and by tolerating it, I was allowing him to imprison me in abuse and unhappy low self-esteem right along with him."

"Recognizing the abuse for what it was finally allowed me to see a ray of sunlight which exposed the walls which had entrapped me without realizing it for many years. I could finally see the confinement for what it was and recognize that if I continued to allow the abuse it would be as if I was my own warden. How could I allow myself to stay in an abusive marriage, and let him keep me in a prison of his own creation when the front door was wide open for me to exit?"

"I had a long way to go and I wasn't perfect – Jack proved right – getting my self-esteem back was a long process. But I could get out because the truth *had set me free. The truth in my case was that I was being emotionally abused and I was no longer willing to tolerate it. So I dared to believe in my dignity, and with the help of a good support system and prayer, I found the strength to act on my dignity and get out of a terrible marriage. I walked out of my prison cell and into a wonderful new life I could never have imagined back then."*

Can An Abusive Marriage Be Saved? Can the Abuser No Longer Abuse?

Not everyone chooses to get out of an abusive marriage by filing for divorce like Claire. Some choose to make a stand and try to save the marriage while working to prevent further abuse from occurring. This is extremely difficult but it is possible. Both positions stem from the same source – the abuse victim must resolve that tolerating any further abuse will no longer be acceptable.

Step #1: **Embrace your dignity.** Unless and until you believe you deserve respect because you are a human being with an intrinsic value or worth, it will be difficult to stand up to your abuser and refuse to tolerate any further abuse. Since abuse is devoid of any respect, and an abuser shows no respect for the victim, the only shred of respect that can surface between them must come from the victim. Until respect is reintroduced into the relationship, there will be none, and the abuse will probably persist.

Step #2: **Refuse to tolerate any more abuse and communicate this to your abuser.** Choosing to stay without committing to refuse any further abuse to be perpetrated upon you, opens the door for your abuser to continue the abuse, and it will decimate the little self-worth you're trying to hold onto, if you have any at all.

Abuse ends when the victim wants it to end badly enough, and is willing to walk away from the relationship if it continues.

Step #3: **Don't pin your hopes on their ability to stop on their own.** Some think an abuser might stop abusing when finally aware of the abusive nature of the behavior. Sometimes this is possible, but sometimes it's not. Pinning your hopes on the abuser stopping without also insisting that you will no longer tolerate abuse is not my recommendation.

Your Best Defense If You Choose to Stay
Choosing to stay in an abusive marriage doesn't mean you are choosing more abuse. But it is your responsibility to make sure you are no longer

abused. Your best defense against more abuse is the same as your best offense – your dignity.

One result of abuse and low self-esteem is that it saps our ability to trust our perceptions, and we begin to doubt we have the strength to get out and survive on our own.

Some abuse survivors are only able to act on their dignity and make the first move toward restoring their self-worth and ending the abuse after enduring one final confrontation or abusive episode with their abuser.

Part of my personal redemption relates to my experience with

ZSA ZSA

As she sat on the opposite side of the bar from me, I tried to figure out which celebrity she resembled.

She was wearing a blue silk blouse and large, flashy gold, jewelry. Her blonde hair was swept up off her neck in an elegant style. As I drank my cognac, we exchanged a few glances, and I kept wondering who this beautiful creature reminded me of. Was she a celebrity? Who was this woman?

I ordered a second drink and walked over to her side of the bar. When I heard her speak, I knew immediately who she looked like and spoke like – Zsa Zsa Gabor. Her looks were eerily similar and she spoke in the same heavy, exotic accent.

"Drinking alone?" I asked.

"Yes."

"Are you married?"

"My husband's in Jerusalem," she responded in her thick accent.

"Mind if I sit?"

"Of course." Although she introduced herself, I never actually got her name. I didn't care. She was Zsa Zsa

Gabor to me, and she'd already told me everything I needed to hear or cared to know. She was alone, her husband was "overseas", and she was drinking alone in a bar in 1973. She'd been making sexy eyes with me for the last 20 minutes.

The next morning as we sat at her small kitchen table making awkward small talk over coffee, her telephone rang. It was only a few feet away on the kitchen wall and Zsa Zsa stood to answer. "Hello?"

She put her hand over the receiver, looked at me and whispered, "It's my husband."

"Your husband?" I responded.

"Yes. He'll be here in a few minutes."

"What?! What do you mean a few minutes? I thought you said he's in Jerusalem!"

"Yes, Jerusalem Avenue, schmuck, and he's coming home in a few minutes." She continued talking to her husband, and again put her hand over the receiver and whispered, "He's got a gun."

I immediately went into a full full-blown panic. "What? Jerusalem Avenue!?!?!? You didn't say that last night! I thought you meant Jerusalem, Israel!!!"

That's when my panic began. Next thing I knew, King Kong was banging on the door.

Zsa Zsa lived in a walk-up apartment on a fairly busy commercial street. It was a small apartment with no back door, and she motioned to the window overlooking the alley below. It was clear that I had *only two options – face an irate, armed husband, or jump. As I stood at the tiny squirrel-sized window, contemplating and panicking, I heard him trying to get into the apartment. Zsa Zsa kept the chain lock on the door, which infuriated him. I heard him threatening her and kicking the door. He was really kicking hard and I knew the door was about to break. I figured I'd rather have two broken legs than end up dead.*

So I jumped.

Fortunately, she only lived on the second floor so the fall wasn't as terrible as it could've been. I aimed for a small patch of grass and landed on it.....well, at least half of me did. Miraculously, I wasn't terribly hurt and I was still alive! Adrenaline pumping, I raced like hell all the way back to my office. I never looked back at the window but I heard lots of shouting.

My secretary was already at the office when I arrived, disheveled and completely out of breath. She never asked a single question or said a word. She simply poured me a cup of coffee and went back to her typing. I dug out a clean dress shirt I kept hanging in a storage closet, and spent the rest of the day full of anxiety and exhausted.

I never heard from Zsa Zsa or her husband again, but I did wonder if it was time to quit drinking and begin my own redemption.

I tell clients about my experiences as a cheater to let them know that I've been there. And that's why I'm including my all-time worst, most embarrassing, outrageous, despicable cheating story here. I get it. I've cheated and I've been cheated on. I know the pain of each situation, and understand what emotions each engender.

Rationalization

It was a harder decision not to rationalize my reasons for cheating, and blame the women I was married to, than it was to make the decision to jump out the window.

Rationalization is a major issue for those who cheat, because it's about externalizing responsibility for your actions and escaping blame. Cheaters already feel so bad about their behavior that accepting any more blame or fault seems too overwhelming. So the easiest thing to do is blame our spouses for "driving us into the arms of another".

When you listen carefully to each person's rationale that led him or her astray, the old common denominator of a "damaged self-esteem" seems a factor in almost every case. The real issue is that the innocent non-cheating spouse, or the one who didn't cheat, is blamed for somehow making the cheater feel inadequate as a person, or unworthy of gratifying sexual experiences and proper physical attention.

When a spouse makes us feel unworthy, unloved, undeserving of our respect, trust, time, attention, or physical affection, our self-esteem takes a big hit. Over time, it's no wonder we get tired of feeling low about ourselves… and begin looking elsewhere for validation and sexual gratification. The cheating spouse is actually saying to the non-cheating spouse, *"I am angry and resentful toward you for the damage you have caused to my self-esteem, and I went outside the marriage to find someone else who would make me feel worthy and valuable in all the ways you don't."*

When we don't feel happy within ourselves, and we get to a point where we can't stand this unhappiness, we do a lot of dumb, risky things just to recapture lost happiness and the euphoria of good self-esteem, if only for an instant. Cheating is an easy, fun, and pseudo vengeful way of experiencing this. It's easy because sex is so readily available in our society. It's fun because that's just the inherent nature of sex. And it's pseudo vengeful because it's our way of "getting back at our spouse" for making us feel "so low about ourselves" that we go out to hurt our partner in some way like they've hurt us – even if we go to great lengths to be sure he or she never find out about our affairs.

Why Rationalizing is Dangerous for Your Self-Worth

Self-introspection and self-honesty is what you must do in order to recapture your self-worth. How can you know what or where you're lacking if you don't have the guts to look within, survey your territory, and figure out how to improve? This can't happen if you continue to assign blame elsewhere or use your spouse as a scapegoat for your own misdeeds and bad behavior. Nobody is responsible for your actions but you.

Infidelity is never about the third party. It's not even about your spouse. It's really about you. People cheat because they feel badly about themselves and they want someone to help them feel better.

Until you can look within, recognize your dignity, and act in accordance with your intrinsic value, you'll always be reliant on others to make you feel good about yourself – so stop blaming others for your bad behavior which erodes your self-respect, self-worth, and self-esteem!

My advice is to avoid the rationalization exercise. Face the music, and take full responsibility for your actions. It is really pitiful to listen to these rational clients try to justify bad behavior. Blaming others for your own mistakes is easy, and if you have someone who will accept this behavior and turn it into a personal problem, it will work every time.

Chapter 6

Physical Divorce

If physical divorce were a breakfast buffet, I've sampled all the dishes – and no two taste the same. In my two failed marriages and one failed ten-year relationship, I've experienced physical divorce from every angle. One thing I've learned is that physical divorce takes you where it finds you.

In 1961, physical divorce found me. Pat and I had been living in Miami while I was attending law school. The process of physically disengaging from her wasn't terribly difficult, though it was heart-wrenching to leave without my precious first-born daughter Stacey. But, at that time, fathers were not awarded custody, and I was in no way fit to be the parent she deserved.

In 1978, physical divorce found me on two separate occasions. The first time was in April after Gretchen and I attempted to make things work during a trip to Florida. The trip was so miserable for us both that I left as soon as we got home. But the physical agony and guilt over the physical separation of my children brought me home. I couldn't stand myself and drank very heavily during my time away. I had to go home and try the marriage again.

After attempting a short two week reconciliation, I left again – for good. During that time I realized the marriage was dead in every way except physically, and learned living under the same roof does not a marriage make.

And, nearly ten years later, physical separation found me again. It was 1989, and after discovering my girlfriend was no longer committed to the relationship, I told her we needed to part company.

Sometimes a joint physical address is the only thing keeping two people united. In those cases, a physical divorce can be a matter of dividing up the paperclips and moving out, while in other cases, it can be an enormously traumatizing event when a person is suddenly dumped without warning.

But no matter where physical divorce finds you, it's important to remember one thing – done wrong, physical divorce can have serious financial, legal, emotional, and psychological consequences.

For some, the physical de-unification of divorce is what terrifies them most when contemplating leaving a marriage. Some people stay only because they are too scared to live alone, or heaven forbid, die alone. Others feel giddy when they think about the physical divorce and are excited by the physical freedom and separation it will provide. As I've grown older, I've witnessed a few friends who regretted staying in unhappy, unhealthy marriages for too long, and now feel obligated to stay when their spouse has contracted a disease or illness.

Using physical divorce as a way of affirming it's time to leave the marriage means you "fast-forward your tapes" of *The Movie of Your Life*, and imagine yourself still physically married years from now. I also encourage imagining yourself divorced years from now. If this is hard for you, rewind the tapes of your life and marriage from your wedding day to the present. How have you changed? How has your spouse changed or not changed? Has the physical union deteriorated or grown during that time? How will yesterday's trends dictate tomorrow's? Have you physically changed since the wedding? Are you seeing things in your spouse you weren't aware of until you were physically residing together? Would it be harder to leave now or later?

Although I hadn't thought of my *Movie of Your Life* metaphor yet, in retrospect, it's obvious I was "fast-forwarding my tapes" when I made the decision to end my first marriage. And I used physical separation first to see if the marriage could be saved. If I'd been using the movie metaphor at the time, I would've said there was neither tape fast-forwarding or rewinding, but rather the movie of my future life was playing live before me every day. It was all I needed to see to affirm that the marriage had to end.

Pat was 18 when I married her. My age matched my bank account balance – I was 20 years old with $20 to my name. With no money, other than wedding gifts, we moved to Coral Gables to complete my senior year at the University of Miami.

Pat was gorgeous and had worked as a model both before and after our twenty-two month marriage. She was warm and had a terrific sense of humor. Like me, Pat loved to sing and her voice was sensational. She was special, but I had no idea what marriage meant or required. All I knew is I wanted to be with her and start a family. The other thing I didn't know when we married, was just how God-awful her mother was. Where my mother was sweet, her mother was sour. Where mine was gentle, she was abusive. I watched numerous occasions of her abusing her husband, Pat's father, yelling about how he did this or that wrong. She was always questioning him, berating him, and humiliating him. It was very upsetting to see him treated this way. He was a wonderful man and a respected physician. From what I saw, he deserved none of this awful treatment but always provided a wonderful home and means for his large family.

Nothing enraged her more than yours truly. She COULD NOT STAND me. Her need to control everyone and everything was beyond comprehension.

She was constantly trying to control me by controlling Pat, often defying my opinions or directions simply to exert authority and force Pat to choose sides. In one shameful encounter, she was relentlessly undermining and bad-mouthing me to Pat. I became so irate that I actually got right in her face and yelled back in the same tone and volume she was yelling at all of us. I am not proud of this, nor was I ever. It was the ultimate battle of the wills but the only thing I remember coming of it was my decision to find a way get Pat and I away from her nefarious influence.

Despite my best efforts to convince Pat to stay with me, two months after enrolling in law school, she returned to New York to reunite with her mother. At 19, Pat was devoid of any self-esteem or ability to make her own decisions after a lifetime of being controlled and manipulated by the ultimate dictator. Jessie had kept her so dependent that it was nearly unfathomable for Pat to genuinely consider staying with me. As much as I didn't want to leave her, divorce was inevitable.

Without me around, Jessie's voice was the only one in Pat's ear. In my case, physical divorce was a mere formality. After three months apart, it wasn't terribly difficult to deal with the separation from her and I was downright giddy to get away from Jessie. Without money or material possessions and assets, there was no property to divide. So, physical divorce took me where it found me – miles away.

Laura

Laura confessed to me that her reason for ending the marriage was what she saw after fast-forwarding the movie of her life. She said, "I sat in my chair facing him one night as he watched television and realized my husband was unaware that I was even in the room. In my tapes, I saw myself sitting in that same chair with this man in 20 years still feeling like I was ghost. I didn't matter at all to him other than giving him sex, cooking his meals and ironing his shirts."

"As much as I was terrified of living alone and having to find a job to support myself, I knew it was even more frightening to risk spending any more time with him, and ending up as empty and bitter as the old woman I saw in my movie. I loved him dearly and adored our home. Walking away from him physically was the hardest part."

"He was the only man I'd ever been with sexually, and on the outside, it looked like I had it all. But after doing everything I could to work on the self-esteem issues and the marriage, in the end, contemplating the physical divorce is what saved me. I knew that leaving everything I loved was the beginning of loving myself."

Laura spent months working with her husband to save the marriage using my advice, and they sought couples counseling. She eventually faced the truth that he was unable or willing to change. In her *earlier efforts, Laura told me she saw herself sitting next to him covered in grand-children and being happy. But when he showed little signs of paying attention to her dignity, integrity or self-esteem, the scenes from the tape changed. Most importantly, as her self-esteem increased, she started paying more attention to the person she was in those scenes from the future.*

As Laura learned to discover the person she was in the present, she had a better idea of the person she wanted to be in the future, and sitting in that chair, in that living room, with that man, wasn't what she wanted. She wanted a man who was interested in her, paid attention to her and was willing to grow.

However, not everyone feels like Laura. Some are so full of anger, resentment, mistrust, or other negative emotions, they are unable or unwilling to separate their emotions from the decision to leave. If you identify with this, and are so looking forward to getting away from your spouse physically, my advice is to do exactly what Laura did.

Laura was smart and dignified because she counted the cost of leaving. Counting the cost of leaving a marriage, a home, material items, etc. can be very expensive, both financially and emotionally. This is why counting the cost is so critical when deciding to end a marriage. It's not good enough to allow emotions to fuel our departure unless we've thought our situation through rationally.

She weighed her fear and unwillingness to leave physically against the costs and benefits of what she'd lose or gain. The cost calculation affirmed that as much as she wanted to stay with him physically, it was too expensive. She used physical divorce to confirm leaving the physical comforts of her home and relationship were worth the emotional, social, psychological, and financial costs. It is extremely important to count the cost of leaving.

I recommend thinking critically about everything the physical de-unification represents. This woman knew divorce wasn't just about physical separation and took the time to ensure her decision was the best one for her.

My best advice is to fast-forward your tapes, think about what you want when you're 80 years old and looking back on the life you led. Try to live your life now so your later regrets will be minimal. Try to avoid concentrating on the short-term headaches and hassle of physically leaving the marriage.

In today's consumer culture, people accumulate far more stuff than we did in the past, and this can make the challenge of physically separating your belongings from your spouse, and extricating yourself physically from the marriage very daunting. But short-term headaches are a poor excuse for blocking you from long-term gains.

People, Places, and Things – The Nouns of Physical Divorce

Physical divorce is not just about people – it's about leaving your house if it gets sold, or you're the one who doesn't keep it, and it's about the redistribution of things. The one inescapable truth is that your environment will change. How drastically depends on your individual situation which includes choices and circumstances beyond your control. The sooner you can accept this, the better.

Who Gets What?
In most states, marital property includes the house, cars, jewelry, interspousal gifts, real estate holdings, collections, boats and/or any other item purchased or acquired during the marriage. In community property states, all community property is split 50/50 while in equitable distribution states like Florida you begin with the premise that each spouse is entitled to half of all marital property absent justification for an unequal distribution.

The Logistics of Stuff Separation
After you and your spouse, or your attorneys have worked out the details of who gets what in the settlement, it's still a good idea to protect yourself from any liability in case you are accused of intentionally damaging or "misplacing" the items that are going to your soon-to-be ex. I recommend taking photos of everything just as it is – all the clothes in the closet, books or DVD's, etc. Take pictures of anything valuable so you have proof that it was the movers, not you, who broke that expensive Tiffany vase. Some people even take videos of themselves walking through the house and packing their ex's items with care. Make sure that all photos and videos are date and time stamped.

Possessions Do Not Equate to Happiness
In the digital age, figuring out who gets the photos, home videos and other records of family memories is less dramatic than it was when I went through my divorces. Each of you can keep copies of all the photos by taking the originals to get scanned or digitized.

I know a man whose wife left him after 20 years together. She was so desperate to get away from him that she left every single thing she owned behind – she didn't even take her toothbrush. This man was stunned to come home and find she wasn't there. She never left a note, and she refused to answer her cell phone despite his countless calls. He told me he was in the middle of leaving another voicemail when the doorbell rang and the process server handed him the divorce papers. He was shocked and devastated.

"The shock of losing my wife was almost too much for me to bear. I'd never experienced such a blow, and I was surprised how emotionally unprepared and ill-equipped I was to handle things. I thought I was a tough guy until this happened.....I'd served in the military, I flew airplanes, and I'm a real man's man. I thought I could deal with anything. But I could not handle changing anything about our house. I kept everything exactly how she'd left it for almost 18 months until my divorce lawyer and a close friend insisted that I see a therapist. Jack was beside himself with how much my delays were costing in temporary spousal support and stuff, but I didn't care.....I was in total denial about everything. It was a comfort for me to come home and see that the house was unchanged. I liked living among her clothes, shoes, and books. But my therapist made me realize my home had become a shrine of a marriage which had long been dead. It took a while but eventually I agreed to discard three items a week so I could reclaim the house as my own. It was easy to do since my wife wanted nothing of what she'd left behind and I think that's what hurt me most.....it seemed she had discarded me, along with all the memories and personal items that she'd accumulated during our marriage. It was like a total rejection of everything we'd ever shared."

"Since I didn't have to worry about packing her stuff, I moved it all into a guest room and then once that room got full, I moved the excess into the guest bathroom. My therapist, and Jack, said that they were eventually seeing me "thaw out" and begin to accept the divorce and deal with the legal issues and emotional trauma in a healthy, productive way. I wasn't perfect, but I was finally starting to feel so much better. The one thing I never understood in therapy was the doctor's insistence that beneath the anger was a tremendous sadness. I didn't deny I was sad, but I was much more enraged than anything else."

"Strangely enough, one night I was moving a collection of glass figurines into the guest bathroom and one of them dropped and shattered on the tile floor. Something about hearing the shattering glass caught my attention, and I started throwing the other figurines as hard as I could against the shower walls, the mirror, the toilet, and the floors. In the middle of my throwing, the anger was so intense that something shocking happened.....I started to cry. And I mean SOB. I cried for a really long time and as much as I tried to stop, I couldn't."

"My therapist was right about having sadness under the anger, and I couldn't believe how much better I felt when I let it all out. It was like a weight had been lifted off me. The next morning as I walked past the huge mess of destruction spilling out of the guest bathroom I thought, 'Well, it's all destroyed and I'm still standing. I can survive this.' The next day my maid spent several hours sweeping up the mess and I was happy to come home to a house that was starting to look more appropriate for the bachelor I was becoming."

This man made important strides once he managed to change the environment which was helping him stay emotionally frozen. I thought the therapist's suggestions in this case were fantastic and I endorse them here. But they aren't for everybody. Some people do better getting rid of everything all at once. In this man's case, that would've been less effective because he'd shown that a sudden or shocking change in circumstance had adverse emotional and psychological effects.

When you've been dumped or if you discover during the divorce that your spouse has already moved on to another romantic partner, it can be very difficult to deal with it emotionally when you are lying in bed at night all alone. It feels unfair that he or she is already in the arms of another, and you might be imagining some kind of bedroom acrobatics your ex is engaging with, as you lie under a heap of your snot-filled tissues in your holey underwear.

My recommendation is to let yourself feel all the sadness, anger and rejection.....let it all come out. Feel betrayed, cry, punch the pillows, get upset. Let it all out. He or she may have beat you to "get a new sex partner", but you're the one who's doing the hard work of dealing with your feelings to improve the odds of your next romantic relationship being healthy and working out.

My recommendations of how to use physical divorce to expedite your emotional and psychological divorce – buy a new mattress, buy new linens, buy new pj's and underclothes. Change your routine. Redecorate your bedroom.

You should experiment with what works for you. The gradual progression of letting go of physical symbols of your marriage might work for some, while others need a radical release of material items. I've had clients tell me their progression in physical divorce mostly mirrored how they were faring in the other mini-divorces. The more you let go, the more you let go. The more you hold on, the more you hold on.

Feeling Stuck?
Physical divorce has the potential to set people free or keep them trapped in the marriage, even years after the divorce is finalized. Sometimes keeping the house can prevent a person from progressing through the appropriate stages of loss and grief, which delays the emotional and psychological divorce. These people aren't forced to physically confront the changes in their lives when they come home to the same address each night and sleep in the same bed.

This can be particularly challenging when your ex has moved out but most of his or her stuff is still hanging in your closet, cluttering the bathroom cabinets, etc.

Silent Darkness
Anyone who's been through divorce knows the loneliest times are often at night. This is true whether you're the dumper or the dumpee. It's a big adjustment to sleep alone after years of listening to your ex snore, spooning as you both doze off, or simply sharing a nightly routine. Lying there in

your ratty bed clothes imagining your ex snuggled up to a hot blonde with perky boobs or a stallion with a six-pack can really increase your anguish. Try not to lose hope! I have good news.

Psychotherapists suggest that imagining your ex sleeping with a new person might not be such a bad sign. Instead some say it's a sign you're making good progress emotionally because it indicates you're not in denial.

One of my hopes for you, is that this book will provide helpful insight into your emotions. Della was a client who had an especially difficult time moving past her pain. She was very bright and very strong, but her pace and ability to handle the divorce was almost too good. I suspected she might be so focused on the details and paperwork in her case that she was ignoring the emotional stuff. During one meeting I gently asked her if I was right, and she exploded in tears. I was shocked. Through her sobs, she explained that every time she laid her head on the pillow, she imagined him with his mistress at her house. Della confided to me that nighttime was "sheer torture". What she said taught me an important lesson. In truth, you don't know what's going on in that new relationship. The new fling could be abusive or worse. But that new relationship is a Band-Aid which temporarily keeps the pain of the wound at bay.

These are the moments you can feel at your lowest low.....thinking he or she is just throwing you away and wondering what the new guy or gal has that you don't. The answer? About two hundred pounds of useless, emotionally warped baggage. You are moving forward in those moments even if you don't think that's true.....you are the one crying and experiencing the pain, working through the emotional and psychological aspects of divorce while your ex is sleeping with the cheap, temporary Band-Aid. You have to let it go. Refusing to allow yourself to feel the pain in these dark moments can put you in jeopardy for having more moments like this in your future.

The Predators of Physical Divorce

Prevent Being Robbed of Net Worth and Self-Worth

How we handle the physical divorce usually reflects how well or unwell we are handling the other mini-divorces, particularly emotional divorce. Our actions announce who we are and where we are in the effort to disengage from our spouse. Fighting over the stuff, denying the changes which must occur in your environment (or have already occurred), and/or destroying marital or personal property belonging to your ex, are the metaphorical equivalent of operating a bank with no security or closed doors. You're practically inviting the robber inside, and risking the loss of all your loot!

The good news is that if you're divorcing with dignity, you'll be much less vulnerable to being robbed. This is because you're committed to moving through the emotions, disengaging physically, and focusing on the person you want to be in the future. If you aren't divorcing with dignity or making solid efforts to deal with your emotions in divorce, how are you building up your self-awareness and self-worth to prevent a robbery? The recovery of self-esteem is like hiring security guards, installing cameras, and dead bolting doors. If you don't do this, the predators or robbers will sense it and attack. They will use everything they know about you, coupled with what they're seeing now. It's not hard to figure out which door to walk through to rob you blind.

Pre-Planners – When to Leave and When to Stay

There are a variety of reasons why a couple should or shouldn't continue to live in the same home during divorce or during reconciliation attempts. It is highly dependent on the people, circumstances and even the laws of the state in which they live. Here are my suggestions about what to consider:

Statistics show if one person moves out of the home during a reconciliation attempt, he or she is more likely to divorce. Remaining in close proximity really forces a couple to determine how and if they can renegotiate their relationship and gives some the peace of mind that comes from the knowledge they gave their all to save the marriage.

There are cases where separating is the only way a person with low self-esteem, or a person who's suffered spousal abuse, can gain the strength to leave for good. A client once told me it wasn't until he got out from under their roof that he could get the perspective he needed to see "just what an abusive, malignant, bitch-faced, evil whore bag my wife really was." He said that living with her had "stripped him of the ability to think about his own needs because she constantly demanded so much attention and work that he never had time to realize just how miserable he was."

Getting away from the home was like breathing fresh air for the first time and all that oxygen in his brain really woke him up.

But living together is a bad idea when it causes such intense animosity that a couple fights viciously and becomes more enraged and resentful with each passing day. I also don't recommend it in abusive situations or where the well-being of your children is negatively affected. It can be confusing for a child to learn their parents are divorcing but continue to live together unless the parents explain why this is so.

Staying under the same roof doesn't have to be a permanent arrangement. There are reasons why it might start out as an acceptable arrangement and then become unhealthy or detrimental as time passes. So just because it's alright initially, don't be afraid of making adjustments when circumstances change.

Lila's case was the classic example of why people coming out of dictator marriages, or who are trying to rebuild a self- esteem that's been decimated, can be a bad idea.

Lila

"Jack advised that living together during the divorce would be very difficult for me, given my husband's controlling nature and the verbal and emotional abuse I'd suffered for so many years. But I thought it was the best decision for our daughter who still lived at home, and because I was terrified about our finances."

"Our average power bill was $500 per month and it had been a long time since we hadn't struggled to find money to keep our lights on. I feared kicking him out would result in losing access to some money to keep our bills paid. But after two months of having to see him every day and listen to his controlling, domineering bitching and criticism of me, I realized Jack was right."

"My self-esteem was about the size of a tiny pea, and having him around made it impossible for me to recover any more of it. Even though my resolve to divorce him was strong, he was intolerant of me becoming an integrated person acting on my dignity. I knew, without the environment which would afford me the opportunity to be myself and act in my and my children's best interests, I was in danger emotionally."

"He'd been resistant to the divorce, so I figured out a way to use physical divorce to make myself clear while still hopefully getting his financial contribution for the house. I kicked him out and told him he could live on the boat docked out back."

"I felt much better after that. My daughter could still see him every day but I didn't. A huge wave of empowerment came over me as I watched him wheel a few suitcases across the back yard and onto the boat. It was awesome seeing one of the zippers burst and all of his underwear burst out of the bag and fall into the water. I laughed like hell as I stood up in MY bedroom watching him curse and yell and throw the other suitcases and clothes onto the boat. I think this is when he finally realized I was serious about the divorce and I was no longer willing to be controlled by him. Boy was he mad."

Chapter 7

Emotional Divorce

Good Grief
Grief is misunderstood and terrifying! But like any other life challenge, the more you know about your challenger, the easier it is to come out on the winning side.

Five Stages: The late Dr. Elisabeth Kubler-Ross's well-researched book, *On Death and Dying,* describes five stages of grief: denial, anger, bargaining, depression, and acceptance. Studies have found these stages are universal for many different life traumas and losses. Grief-stricken people don't travel through each stage in an orderly progression. Everyone's path is different. But most of us experience each stage at some point during our process of grieving and adjusting to the major life changes brought on by divorce.

Denial Is the Worst: Of the five stages in the Kubler-Ross model, I have observed for most people, the denial stage is the most pervasive and counter-productive. It can linger way too long. It is like a blindfold which both protects you, and comforts you in a dysfunctional way. Being in denial is like staying in bed all day with the covers pulled over your head – like a child with his fingers in his ears, and eyes squeezed shut, yelling, "Na-na-na-na…" It's like a drug used to soothe and zone out, and it can be addictive.

Dumpees: Dumpees are the ones who discover their marriages are over after being blindsided by a shocking revelation or announcement. They are the ones who usually experience denial and disbelief for an inordinate length of time. Denial that drags on too long keeps you from accepting the truth about your situation, legal options, and financial mess. You need to move past this denial stage so you can make the best decisions for your future.

Dumpers: You have been secretly contemplating divorce for some time, and have already worked through your denial that the marriage is over. Whatever initiated the death throes of the relationship, you are most likely the clear-headed one. This puts you at an advantage in the settlement negotiations. Even though you might still be experiencing sadness, you most likely are ready to move on with your life. You have accepted the situation, and can think clearly about your options. This helps you communicate more efficiently with your attorney, come to a fair settlement, and "win" in the battle for dignity, self-worth, and net worth.

Going through the stages of grieving puts you on a roller coaster of emotions. You are reeling and dizzy from the denial, anger, bargaining, depression, and acceptance and in a big blur of confusion. Try to compartmentalize each unpleasant revelation as it comes along. This will make your emotional divorce less overwhelming. If you track your progress and each victory, small or large, it will empower and encourage you to continue finding the strength you need to move forward.

The grief process entails "rocking back and forth between the stages of grief." One moment you are accepting an aspect of your situation and the next minute something happens and you're back in denial all over again.

My client, Lila, likened the emotional rollercoaster of grief and divorce to being in a snow globe. She said, "Jack, you know those snow globes that you buy in a touristy gift shop? Those things you shake and twist or turn upside down and the white snowflakes whip and whirl all around as they flutter in the globe? That's how it feels every time a new revelation is made or a 'pit viper' attacks me during this divorce. I feel like my whole world gets turned upside down and everything I thought I had a handle on emotionally, financially, or psychologically goes back into chaos once again. It is so discouraging and disheartening. It feels like this is never going to end and that I can't control or foresee when someone is going to come along and shake things up next."

"It's tough for me, because one day I'd be fine.....dealing with life, figuring out how to pay our $500 light bill by eating scrambled eggs and toast for a week.....going to work.....conducting things as best I could. I'd go to bed feeling pretty good, all things considered, but in the morning after my snowglobe was shaken and flipped, I might not be able to get out of bed – the grief, sadness and anxiety overwhelmed me, and I literally didn't think I was going to be able to put my feet on the ground. I'd lie in bed as long as I could staring up at the ceiling, or curled up in a fetal position thinking about my frustration. I never knew how I was going to feel from one day to the next, and when I had days like this, I thought I was regressing.....that I wasn't making any progress to overcome it all emotionally."

"It wasn't until my divorce was nearly finalized that I discussed this with Jack. I wish I'd known sooner what I experienced was natural and normal. The thing that saved me was my children. They were THE ONLY REASON I could actually put my feet on the floor most every morning."

Lila's analogy about the snowglobe is both poignant and precise. There are all kinds of new, awful events which occur during divorce and, as Lila suggested, they kick up all the snow around us, and it can take weeks for things to settle back down. But they don't have to set us back entirely in our emotional divorce or other early stages of divorce, if we don't let them. These snow globe episodes are painful because the new problems or discoveries trigger and intensify all the emotions that divorce already stirred up within us. When the snow globe gets tipped upside down, these new discoveries or issues usually force us to revisit painful emotions or issues we thought we dealt with already, or are still struggling with. The grief process seems to be compounding.

My advice is to follow Lila and stick to your dignity plan to deal with the grief, and manage the aftershocks of a snow globe disaster. Lila found a way to move forward no matter how slowly she moved, or how small the steps.

For her, it was a refusal to give up because of her children that motivated her to keep getting out of bed every morning.

You must find something.....anything.....to keep putting your feet on the ground during the grieving process. Get up, if only to feed your children breakfast, walk the dog, meet a friend for coffee, or go scream at your divorce attorney.....something! Literally putting your feet on the floor and getting dressed is baby-stepping your way through the grief!

So just keep going. You are healing and dealing, and soon, you'll see just how far you've grown and overcome through your grief, and this will really boost your self-esteem!

Daring to Detox from Denial

I'm all about truth. Accepting the truth is never easy, especially if you've been avoiding or denying it for years, and it doesn't just happen overnight. It's a painful process, and coming "off of" denial is like detoxing from a drug or alcohol. Substance abusers get "clean" physically well before they get "clean" emotionally. Underlying pain, problems, and dysfunction of life are at the root of all addictions. Once the drug is removed, these issues come to the surface and must be dealt with "sober". It is exactly this same process when coming out of denial. You have to take off the blindfold, get out of bed, take your fingers out of your ears, and finally, squarely meet the truth head-on. In this sense, divorce can be like going to "rehab" – painful and terrifying, but ultimately in your best interest. Even if your divorce is the last thing in the world you want, you must face reality.

"Then you will know the truth and the truth will set you free." (John 8:32)

Daring to detox from denial isn't the most fun experience in life, largely because when we start seeing glimpses of the truth in our life, we don't like what we see. We don't like what that truth means for how our life will change. But at least we're finally seeing things for what they are, and this is big progress! When I see clients experiencing detox, it usually signals a change in our meetings about their case.

One client who was steeped in denial, spent months refusing to accept even the tiniest, most benign morsels of truth about how her life was going to change financially because of the divorce. Her husband had hidden all his money offshore in the Cayman Islands and she had no money to hire an investigator to track it. So for months she'd become enraged, having such indignant tantrums in my office because no progress was being made in her case. Finally, she showed a glimmer of progress in her divorce because gradually, she started to listen and ask questions such as "What if?" These "what ifs" were a signal to me she was starting to process the truth.....daring herself to think about how her life would be if I were telling her the truth. Rather than living in the cave of denial, and losing time and momentum, she slowly was able to begin the process of strategizing, planning, and building a great case. But at first, she couldn't help me help her, because she was absolutely buried in denial.

After we settled her case, she came to see me. She said, "Jack, I was just so fearful of what was going to happen in my life I couldn't accept the truth of what you were saying, or what anyone else in my life was trying to tell me. I didn't want to hear that I'd have to start working after 35 years out of the workforce. I didn't want to hear I'd have to sell my Jaguar and my house. I didn't want to hear that my children would have to apply for financial aid at their universities in order to continue their education. But you were right, I had to experiment with what it would be like to accept just one of these truths at a time. I couldn't just accept the horror of my changing life circumstances all at once. It was just way too overwhelming. So once I took one piece at a time, I could finally dare to detox from denial and make some progress."

Unbelievably, some people tell me that they "can't go there", that is, into the truth, because they "don't have the time". Folks, you need to make the time because your divorce demands it. You have to push through the fear and wake up to the reality of your marital divorce issues, and the emotional agony underlying your entire life experience right now, in order to score the most successes in the divorce. Divorcing with dignity, and dignifying your emotions as a human being by acknowledging and accepting those emotions is really the only ways to survive it – and get something out of it!

Yes! That's right. Divorce is the transition period in life that actually allows us to see what we've "won" on D-day or decree day. Unlike the grief that comes from a death of a loved one, there's an actual "end" date or "finality date" of divorce, on which you can reflect back and see just how far you've come. The difference between people who get the most in divorce and feel the best, and those who don't, is that the winners found the courage to face THE TRUTH. The truth set them free to move out of the pain and the past, and take big giant steps toward happiness and success.

Grief, Truth, and the Battle for Net Worth

The thing about grief is that it keeps us from accessing the full range of options and choices which really are available to us. It keeps us rigid and inflexible. We can only accept a few truths and ignore or deny the rest. This means we go into our divorce settlement negotiations in the worst possible bargaining position – we are fearful and reactive, rather than calm and responsive.

If you are lingering in denial, desperate to feel better but unable to face the truth, you are vulnerable to grab on to anything external and tangible for comfort.

Denial prevents you from accepting anything other than what you want to see. You are so afraid of losing one single penny because you NEED it so much more than you realize. The money is what you think will make your life a success and make you feel better.

Our odds for success on the battlefield of self-worth are greatly diminished when we haven't dealt with our emotional grief. There's no amount of money in the world that can "compensate" us for our anguish the way we hope it will. When we focus exclusively on the battle for net worth, we fail to acknowledge the importance of our self-worth. You won't get as much as you want, or feel as good about what you're getting when you continue to ignore your need for self-esteem and dignity. You can't see the extent of your victories when you haven't acknowledged the extent of your defeats!

That's why denial is like a drug.....addicts don't usually recover until they've "hit rock bottom". That's what happened to me that day in the diner in 1978. I hit rock bottom after suffering the loss of two marriages and two sets of children. My shaking hand woke me up to the extent of what I'd lost because of my alcohol problem and denial. Until you can see just how much loss and pain you've suffered, you can't experience the joy nearly as much as you would otherwise.

Yes, winning lots of money in the battle for net worth is awesome. And it's what every divorce attorney wants for their clients. But it's an empty happiness because you had to have it. It was like a "fix" for an addiction you aren't even aware of. And at some point, that money isn't going to be enough for you to continue your habit. It will either run out because you've mismanaged it, or you'll suddenly realize how little happiness or relief it provided. What will you do then?

Dignity Is the Key to Healing

Part of this challenge of divorcing with dignity is dignifying our emotions.....all of them. Even the ones we aren't yet aware of. When we acknowledge and accept our emotions by confronting the truth, we take the first steps toward detoxing and healing. It happens because we stop protecting ourselves from seeing the pain and dealing with it, so we can use the good that can come out of it to our advantage in divorce.

Abuse Victims
Shortly after Lila's divorce was finalized, I received a letter from her sister, Katy, who had accompanied Lila to her first visit to meet me. She wrote,

"The most influential moment for me through Lila's divorce was our very first meeting with you. You knew this man, her abusive husband, down to every little detail. You had an immediate response for every excuse, comment or

question my sister came up with. I left feeling that I was not crazy and not the only one to be dealing with such a horrible person."

One of the lessons I learned from Lila's divorce was just how far-reaching the effects of abuse can be, and the extent to which one person's abuse affects others around that family. Lila wasn't even aware her husband's treatment of her qualified as abuse. His tirades had somewhat desensitized her, but his despicable behavior had significantly impacted her family. Katy suffered years of anguish as a result of her brother-in-law's abusive nature as she too, was a target of his vitriolic tirades.

Repairing the damage caused by her long marriage has been challenging for Lila, but she still struggles to heal the wounds between her and Katy. She sent me a thoughtful note a few years ago and revealed that her abusive marriage affected far more people than she'd ever imagined, "It affects people you would never guess, and impacts how others may model their lives."

Lila's letter reinforces how abuse impacts the decisions, behavior, and even lifestyle of those who are subjected to it – even when they aren't direct victims. She was so distraught over how her husband's abuse affected so many of her friends and family that she implored me to write this book and asked me to deliver a message from her to you, Dear reader, *"This is what I want to say to the helpless souls who need hope that there is a better life. You do not need to accept the abuse, and this book can be your first step to getting OUT!"*

You, Your Ex, and Dating

Dealing with Your Ex When You're Dating Someone New
Apply the golden rule! How you behave in this sticky area says far more about who you are and your character than anything else! How would you like it if your ex rubbed your face in a hot and heavy new romance with a fitness instructor? How would you feel watching them grope each other in front of you? It's totally undignified to use a new person as a means to your end of getting revenge or provoking jealousy in your ex. It doesn't value or acknowledge any dignity of any party, so don't do it.

It's all about respect. Respect is really the key issue when it comes to new romantic relationships, co-parents, and children. Everyone always asks me when or how to introduce a new love interest, and my answer is always the same – apply the golden rule and question how you can best show all interested parties that you respect them, as individuals, and where they are in their recovery from divorce. So, treat your soon-to-be-ex the way you'd like to be treated if the tables were reversed.

Sometimes it's impossible to know where anyone is with emotional and psychological divorce. You might think he or she has gotten over you since the divorce was last year and things have been cool and drama-free. Then wham!

You bring your new partner around, and things with your co-parent suddenly go from civil to awful. If the introduction or awareness of your new relationship triggers jealousy or anger, the worst thing you can do is invalidate his or her emotions about it. Telling people how they should feel about your new bliss will usually only make them more angry, hurt and resentful. How they feel is how they feel, and how you feel is how you feel. If you're going to talk about any feelings at all, it should be your regretful feelings about them and your time together.

Sometimes it helps to hear an ex affirm emotions about you and how he or she perceives the years of marriage. For instance, one client once told me that her ex-husband gently thanked her for wonderful children, happy memories, and years of good times together. She said she just needed to hear that he still loved her and he always would and that she'd never be replaced in his heart.

I've heard this on several occasions, and I think it helps resolve one of the core "hangover questions" people often confront after a divorce.....sometimes years later. Whether a divorce is nasty or nice, many spouses later wonder if they have or will be forgotten, if they ever really mattered or were loved, and if their years of matrimony are still "of record" to their ex. When a new relationship develops for an ex and those questions are still unresolved, it can make the adjustment about the new romantic status more challenging.

It matters how your ex feels about your new relationship. Things can get really tough when a co-parent introduces the new significant other to the children before his or her ex is aware of the relationship, or is capable of dealing with it in a dignified manner. It's bad enough to feel like an ex's new partner is a "replacement" of us, but it's ten times worse to confront a new person who threatens to replace us as a parent!

Trust me, it goes a long way when a jealous or unhappy ex asks if the new person has met the kids and your answer is "no". I've found that this question is frequently misinterpreted and the responses much more insightful than most people think. What I mean is that most people overlook what lies at the heart of this question – respect. And at the heart of respect is dignity. When you can answer "no" to this question, it shows respect toward your ex, and your children.

At the very least, you want to show your co-parent your respect as a co-parent. Rushing your new lover over to meet your kids before your ex is aware of the relationship or before your children are ready to deal with this challenge is disrespectful and damaging.

Just because he or she is dating, doesn't mean you should. Doing that whole "tit for tat" thing is unattractive and undignified. Just because your ex has seemingly "moved on from you," doesn't mean it's that way at all.

When Your Ex Starts Dating
When an ex starts dating too early during divorce, or earlier than you think he or she should, it can be very difficult emotionally. Lots of jealousy, envy, resentment, and unresolved anger can cause problems for you and your relationship as co-parents.

How to deal with the emotions? Acknowledging your feelings is the first step toward healing and getting over it. Be okay with how you're feeling about it. Those emotions should be dignified with acknowledgement, acceptance and attention because they are part of you and your human experience. They need to come out and the sooner they do, the better.

Mimi

One client who still struggles with this is Mimi. Mimi's divorce was ten years ago, and she still can't get out of the grief. Mimi's husband was a total jackass – verbally abusive, unfaithful, a recreational drug user, poor businessman, selfish, and greedy.

The decision to divorce came when a series of bad investments left them on the brink of bankruptcy. In a fit of rage, her husband announced he was leaving Mimi for his 25-year-old assistant. If this weren't bad enough, months before this final explosive encounter, Mimi had been diagnosed with a crippling illness for which there is still no cure – her health would continue to deteriorate over time.

As much as I cared about Mimi and liked her, she was a nightmare client. Mimi was extremely difficult to represent because she suffered, and still suffers from, unresolved grief. Mimi was able to move out of denial and accept the truth of her changed circumstances during the divorce, but post-divorce, she hasn't been able to implement the truth of her situation as the foundation for her future and happiness.

Mimi had the courage to face the pain and acknowledge the truth, but she was unable to deal with them properly and release them. It was difficult for me to deal with Mimi because every little thing that went wrong in the marriage, and her case, was all her husband's fault. If she stubbed her toe on the way into my office, it was his fault. If she chipped her nail polish, he was somehow the culprit. Every little problem in their marriage was his fault. She could not take responsibility for her role in anything other than being the patron saint of terrible marriages.

The tragedy of Mimi's story is that she's still stuck in her grief many years later. Her victim mentality keeps her stuck in the past. She can't let go of all the injustices she suffered and acknowledge the present. It's too difficult for her to take responsibility for anything other than her pain, and she blames her ex for causing it. She has alienated everyone in her life...except for me. But I'm getting awfully close to joining the others!

I can't help but want to scream! "Mimi! Your movie is on 'repeat!' You keep watching the same scenes from years ago, and haven't come out of the past! You would have so many more choices, and chances for happiness, if you'd just let go of your victim mentality!" It is so frustrating when a victim just wants to stay a victim.

Please stay alert to your grief process or seek counseling if you suspect you're getting stuck. Divorcing with dignity is about movement, not stagnation. It won't help much to confront the truth if you then lack the courage to do the work necessary to heal from the pain.

Guilt: The Easy Way Out

Sounds hard to believe right? How can feeling guilty in divorce be the easy way out.....guilt sucks!? But guilt is one of those tricky emotions in divorce because it lets you believe intellectually you're doing all the right things. You are not wanting to "rub any more salt" in the wounds your past misdeeds caused, so you're acting in everyone else's self-interest before considering your own. Our brains think, "Hey this is great, I'm finally doing what's right and being the nice guy (or girl). All this selflessness should make up for my past selfishness, right?" Our heads are telling us giving away more money than necessary, or not asking for more money than we're entitled to receive, is the easiest, most convenient way to make up for our sins.

Well, that's what our heads say, but what's going on in our hearts? Our hearts are so full of guilt it's often the only emotion we can identify.

Emotional Divorce – Moving Past Guilt and Self-Esteem
There are many stages of emotional divorce, and it's up to you to dig into that frozen tundra inside so you can move past the guilty stage. Guilt, manifested as narcissism, false ego, or other projections, seriously damages self-esteem, and is what keeps people from seeing the truth and setting themselves free. These guilty people aren't self-aware (a core component of self-esteem) but rather, they're self-deluded.

The difference between those who gain the most and those who don't, is how they deal with the guilt and regret.

Accept what happened and accept what can't be changed
Acceptance is one of the first stages of overcoming guilt because it forces you to be rational about the past. The past is permanent. No amount of apologizing or regret will change your mistakes or erase them, so you file for emotional bankruptcy – for protection from perceived emotional creditors. When are you going to stop paying for them, both financially, and emotionally? Accept them and move forward.

Guilt And The Battle For Net Worth

People who feel consumed by guilt often lose big financially. That's because they try to "buy their way out of it" by agreeing to ridiculous settlements in which they literally "pay for their sins". But this doesn't do what you're hoping it will do, it doesn't make you feel better. Instead it only delays the inevitable – you'll get bitterness.

Deal with your guilt now, before you write a huge check, or you settle for far less money than you might otherwise. It's imperative you deal with the emotions underlying the guilt feelings while the divorce is proceeding, so you can be sure your financial success is everything it can possibly be.

Guilt and Pride
Get over yourself! What kind of power trip are you on?! Phony guilt is a major pride trip. This kind of guilt is all about YOU, and all about the power you had over TWO people in a relationship. What makes you think you had so much power, or that it all hinged on YOU and your actions? Why is it that YOU, and only you, were responsible for the demise of your marriage? Get over yourself.....it wasn't all your fault and that means it isn't all your responsibility to make amends for now.

Self-Respect
When the light bulb comes on, after we get out of a marriage and finally start seeing how badly our self-esteem has been damaged, and when we commit to the hard work of divorcing with dignity, we realize just how much self-respect we lost in our bad marriage. Now, we recognize our values include US as people.....we learn how to value our own life, and our emotional and physical health, more than value the needs of an abusive spouse. We can forgive ourselves for feeling responsible for abuse perpetrated upon us.

The guilt is really a problem because you wonder "how could I have been so devoid of any recognition and failed to honor my own dignity and recognize my inherent value as a human being, that I allowed myself to get so grossly mistreated for so long?!" This is scary when you finally recognize just how little self-respect you once had in your marriage. So rather than continuing to beat yourself up about it, commit instead to doing something about it! How many more years will you let pass without feeling good about yourself!? You might have escaped an abusive marriage, but if you can't get past your guilt, you become your own abuser.....and your full recovery on the self-worth battlefields becomes impossible.

Mary

Mary was a client who experienced years of losses even though she'd won big time in the net worth battle. She was never physically abused, but her ex threatened abuse on several occasions during the marriage. She lived in fear because he'd explode in tantrums sometimes, but his abuses of choice were mostly emotional and economic abuse.

Despite having millions in assets, her ex provided almost no real love, emotional support, or money. After years of marriage and four children, she finally found the courage to leave, and never even said goodbye to anyone. She truly vanished.

Her divorce was pretty nasty – her husband was hurt and resentful about losing any money (although of course he thought his piddly, trifling little settlement offers were more than fair), and Mary was bitter. Her anger and resentment wasn't only directed at her husband, but Mary also felt a mixture of the anger and resentment aimed at herself.

Not every spouse in a divorce who is bitter, experiences this particular kind of self-directed anger. Some of them really do believe they were a "perfect spouse" who "didn't do anything wrong". They believe their ex is to blame for all their problems, and the ex-partner should pay in every possible way to "make it up" to them.

Mary was absolutely riddled with guilt over staying too long, and over the harm it did to her children, etc. So when she won a very impressive victory on the battlefield of net worth, she was happy and pleased, but still terribly encumbered by guilt. Rather than have the ability to truly savor the overwhelming joy on D-day, she could only see all that money as a way to absolve herself from her guilt. Instead of seeking counseling, she tried to buy her way out of the guilt she felt by spoiling her children and grand-children. It took about 15 years for her to lose every penny of her settlement.

Mary was a very sad case because she had to keep self-sacrificing as a way to absolve herself of the mistakes of her past. She kept focusing on the past or the "bad things" about herself, so she was unable to spend the little time each day to look and act on the good that was still possible in her life.

Mary failed to gain any self-worth other than finding the strength and courage to finally leave the marriage. But that's as far as she got. The guilt was so overwhelming, she couldn't break through it to get to the good positive feelings underneath all the unresolved negative emotions.

Getting to the core of who you are and your intrinsic value is about cultivating who you are, and taking the time to really figure out what your gifts are and what makes you happy.

You can't be happy unless and until you begin to honor the value and worth you were given by God and born with. You do a disservice when you don't look into those things, when you don't devote time and energy into cultivating yourself to serve others in their pursuit of living the life they were meant to live. What good are you to help grow, when you haven't done that yourself, and haven't learned the lessons of how to do it? All you're doing to your kids is showing them the consequences of not acting to honor yourself. They respect you less and less, and feel less guilt about taking advantage of you. Why shouldn't they? You don't respect yourself.

Guilt in giving away all your money is a good example of this. When you give it all away out of guilt, you're thinking it's all your fault, that you and your actions were worthless and inexcusable and define you as a person who doesn't deserve anything other than suffering. You let them steal some of your gold in their effort to feel better about themselves by putting you down, and shaming you, and further decaying and destroying your self-respect in order to prop theirs up.

Why Accepting Rationalization Is Bad for Your Self-Worth and Net Worth

One of my last cases before leaving New York and moving to Florida involved Beth, a woman I met at a friend's wedding. Following the ceremony, I was chatting with the other attendees while I waited for the heavy January snow to subside a little so I could safely drive in less than "white out" conditions. As I waited, Beth came up to me and introduced herself and her husband, who was a doctor, and their three children.

She then asked me what I did for a living and I said I was an attorney.

She asked, "What type of law do you practice?" I said, "Divorce law."

She smiled and said, "I'll never need your services."

Beth

Two weeks later, I walked into my New York office and she was sitting in my lobby area. Between my introduction and that meeting, she'd discovered her husband with her best friend, which was heart-wrenching for Beth.

It was no surprise that he continued this pattern of behavior during the divorce. He blamed Beth for everything, and was devoid of any guilt or contrition. Instead, what I witnessed was pure, unadulterated resentment toward his wife, which I can only presume was his justification for the affair he was pursuing. For him this translated to constantly berating Beth throughout the divorce. Indignation and stubbornness, along with personal attacks or sarcasm, were his modus operandi at the settlement conferences.

Since I wasn't his attorney, it was frustrating there was nothing I could do to get him to reconsider his blame role and behavior. All I could do was try to help her recover her damaged self-esteem which had been shattered in the aftermath of discovering his affair, not to mention the years she spent in an unhealthy marriage to this person.

Her husband's pattern was to wear Beth out in order to get what he wanted. If she asked for X, he argued for Y, and If she didn't agree, he would argue relentlessly and yell and insist on why his position was better.

Eventually, Beth would get so exhausted and frustrated she'd relent. Of course his attorney was thrilled with his behavior.

He was just steam rolling over Beth.....well, he would have if I hadn't been there. Beth's self-esteem was so low when we began negotiations, even the rage and betrayal she felt weren't enough to overcome her inability to fight for what she deserved under the law.

She was so angry about the underlying issues in their marriage and the affair, that his belligerence and indignation exacerbated all her negative emotions and fury, exhausting her, and frustrating her so much it was sapping her energy. She was spending so much time and energy in her anger that she didn't have the strength to really think smart and focus on the important issues which directly affected her future.

Once Beth was able to make the decision to divorce with dignity and truly embrace my message, that this divorce and the rest of her life had nothing to do with him and everything to do with her, she was able to begin coping productively with the betrayal issues, etc. and engage in the divorce responsibly. She stopped letting her anger get the better of her, and took some of the emotion out of the business of divorce.

Beth was finally able to rationally comprehend what she was entitled to under the law, stand firm, and not allow him to wear her down or intimidate her anymore. She could now navigate her life much more effectively.

At one of our settlement conferences, after minimal progress due to her husband's continued accusations and blame shifting, as well as Beth's refusal to give in to his atrocious behavior and treatment of her, it was clear we were heading to an impasse. I asked his attorney if I could speak to his client alone. He agreed.

I went into a private room with Beth's husband, and told him all about my own experiences as a philanderer. Sharing my personal history with him caught him off guard, and he asked me why I would share these private details with the spouse of his client. I said, "I was a lot like you at the beginning of my second divorce. I wanted to blame and rationalize all my bad behavior at the expense of my former wife. And we're not alone in struggling with this temptation."

"Almost every man and woman I've represented who has been unfaithful wanted to make excuses for their infidelity by blaming their spouse, because they feel so guilty for what they've done. This guilt is debilitating because it disparages your spouse, further poisons your relationship, and can possibly effect the way your children perceive either of you. Even more debilitating is the self-deception brought on by this guilt."

"Blaming Beth in order to minimize your guilt exacerbates your infidelity fog. When you attempt to characterize your wife as the reason for your unfaithfulness, you are inflicting even more pain on her, yourself, and your children."

"You are making a bad situation even worse which will make you feel worse about yourself, and it's *costing you thousands in attorney's fees because your inability to accept responsibility for your life is a major reason why these negotiations are dragging on. The sooner you accept responsibility for yourself and for your behavior, the sooner you can recover your self-worth, settle your case and move on."*

"I know this is hard to do.....It was actually a harder decision for me not to blame my former wife for my infidelity, than to jump out Zsa Zsa's window that day. But I finally realized that not owning up to my bad behavior, and further hurting my family, was the direct result of my blame shifting."

"I knew the only option was to acknowledge my culpability, to accept that my behavior was wrong, and I would need to face the consequences of my behavior."

"When I look back at the wreckage I caused with my behavior, I had to find my own way to avoid inflicting this type of harm on any other human being for the rest of my life. That's exactly what's needed in order to salvage your own sense of self-respect and end the bitterness."

As a result of that self-effacing experience, we settled their case that day.

Chapter 8

Parenting

Adult Children
Adult children who are faced with divorcing parents are in a unique situation because they usually have a good idea of what went on in the marriage, and have formed their own opinions over the years. No matter how mature, responsible, or insightful you believe your children are, they are still your ex's offspring too. Do your best to avoid speaking negatively or harshly about your ex. No dignified parent wants to be responsible for adding to the wedge which may already exist between a parent and child.

While it feels good to have your kids on your side, comforting and protecting you, you are still the parent. Help them confront their own pain about how this divorce is affecting them. Just because they don't live at home doesn't mean they don't experience an emotional transition when their older parents divorce.

Adopted Children
Divorce is not a license to pick and choose which children you wish to keep. On a few occasions, I've represented parents of adopted children who have delicately expressed interest in continuing to seek custody for the biological offspring, exclusively. I have confronted these individuals with the injustice of their goals.

Absentee Co-Parents
Sometimes it's best when a parent doesn't fight for custody, or fights only for some parenting time. It's painful when the natural parent feels let down

and angry that the other parent seems disinterested in the lives of their children. Be thankful you know where they stand now, so you can protect the children from further pain whenever possible. When your ex fails to live up to your expectations, you and your children suffer if you expect the ex to be the parent your kids need, but is not.

This is a tough experience for kids who are always on the roller coaster of high hopes and gut wrenching lows of disappointment. It is well known that children feel responsible for problems with and between their parents. For example, they blame themselves because they accidentally spilled ice cream in the car during the last visit, or something similar. Kids can learn a lot of negative emotional lessons in situations like this. Internally, they tell themselves, "if I were only better, less clumsy, and more loveable, my parents would still be together, or at least my dad (mom) would want to spend more time with me."

Stability
Research shows the quality of life after divorce is what affects children, not the divorce per se. This means the parents' ability to adjust and maintain stability is terribly important, and the custodial parent must especially have a healthy lifestyle. Some co-parents just can't find stability for their kids. It might be that addictions or low self-esteem prevents them from being the co-parent you and your children deserve. If that's the case, be thankful for what they can and are doing. And believe me, it can sometimes be a real blessing when a parent essentially abandons the child. Sometimes not having him or her around is better for everyone.

Heather

Heather was a client who had suffered the loss of nearly every ounce of self-esteem she ever had because of a bad marriage. She and her spouse fought bitterly over custody of their child, and we eventually lost her case for primary physical custody.

Heather was from Connecticut, and she was so emotionally devastated in every conceivable way, she felt returning to her hometown and family was the best thing she could do. Of course, she intended to return regularly for visits with her son, but she never could improve psychologically or emotionally despite being at home with her loved ones. This resulted in chaos and more emotional turmoil for her son.

She should have committed to visits four times per year for three weeks at a time, and stuck to it. Heather always felt like she wasn't doing enough, and was so overwhelmed by what she thought she wasn't doing, that she couldn't do what she should or could be doing.

Their son suffered because he was in the middle and never was sure what was going to happen. There was no definite plan of when he'd be with her. Her crazy was making him crazy – and infuriating his father. It all came to a head when she eventually kidnapped the child and took him home to Connecticut with her. It was horrible for all involved, and though the child was returned, the damage was done.

Her son felt uneasy with her because she was so flighty, so he was terribly upset about the unsupervised visits with his mother. He couldn't count on her. There is only so much I can do for a client, especially one like this who wants to live far away. Someone in her family or a close friend should've helped her get control or find a therapist. Her son was clearly the victim.

Visitation rules must be clearly articulated and put in writing. If you are the visiting parent, make sure your kids understand there are times when you won't make it at the last minute.....because of traffic or work or something. Explain to them they are your top priority. Be the parent you say you are, or want to be. If you aren't good at it yet, that's okay.....commit yourself to learning. Read books. Find a counselor. Call me. Do something.

Obviously this is a major issue in the development of children's self-esteem and emotional well-being. You can help them by refraining from spreading your own anger or bitterness about your ex. Accept what they are and aren't willing to do. Spend your emotional energy on enriching your children's lives rather than wasting it on bitterness toward your ex.

A Word for Fathers and Custody

As much as most fathers fight like hell for joint or primary custody of their kids, a substantial portion of them also don't really have a clue what they're in for. When I tell them that the custody agreement allows them to have the kids on weekends and a few Wednesdays per month, they look excited, but I can tell many of them have a moment of panic. It's like they suddenly realize they have the kids......alone. Marriage and parenting are designed to be team sports, and when these dads realize they just lost their pinch hitter, they get nervous. How do I make the grilled cheese like Mommy? What do I do when they've had a bad week at school?

If your ex is complaining about your lack of awareness or knowledge about your own children, then graciously accept the "offer" to write a list of everything she knows so you can know it too. Don't let her just wave that guilt over you and then not help you. Your kids might know or suspect you don't have any clue about them, but any opportunity you can get to prove them wrong, the better.

Show them you've boned up and are in the game to stay. Fathers frequently face the tough process of redefining themselves as a parent, and as a man, following divorce. Usually, women are the emotional caregivers of children and the father "gets away" with bringing home the bacon and taking direction from the wife about which child needs an extra hug or a high five. They are able to stay emotionally disengaged because their spouse is there to do what they consider to be the "mom stuff" or the "hard, emotional chores" of meeting their child's needs. Many men think they are great fathers because they provide well, are there each night to tuck them in, and that's it. But now that they have parenting rights, alone, it's time to "parent-up". Each kid needs a close relationship with both parents.

Blended Families and Step-Parenting

Clients and friends refer to me as *"The Dean of Step-Parenting"*. As a biological father to four children from two wives, and a step-father to two children from my third wife Angela, I've found that the road isn't always very smooth. Angela and I have learned a lot from our kids and each other. And it's helped to see how my clients have learned from my mistakes and me from theirs. So this is my best advice…

Angela and I learned the hard way, as well as hundreds of clients, that mutual trust is the biggest part of managing a blended family successfully, and it begins with trusting each other. This requires communication, honesty and a commitment to do what you all agree to do. It's an integral part of being a dignified parent and co-parent. And it's impossible to trust each other when you aren't paying attention to the other's self-esteem.

I've found one of the most troubling problems in blended families is when a dispute arises between a step-parent and a child. As a parent to two beautiful step-daughters during their teen years, I certainly had my share of miserable disputes. Rebellious teenage girls, hormones, boys at the door….. ugh. It can be a nightmare for a step-father.

When disputes arise, it's crucial all the parents together form a united front to the kids, sticking to the rules, being consistent, disciplining fairly, etc. This doesn't mean each parent shouldn't voice his or her opinions. These adult strategy meetings must take place outside the presence of the kids. Children of divorce (and all children) need to know whom to trust, and where the boundaries are. A kid with no clear rules and no discipline, is a kid headed for trouble. So, for their sake, be a team, play fair, and make parenting with dignity everyone's first priority!

I learned the hard way with my biological families, that arguing with a spouse in front of the kids is a bad idea. It erodes the respect the children feel toward the spouse who is constantly undermined and questioned. Trust is compromised, child to parent, and parent to parent. When you fear humiliation because your ex makes you look like an insignificant or less meaningful parent/adult in the eyes of the biological children, you'll disengage over time – feeling like your contributions aren't appreciated.

Step-parenting isn't just about survival, it's about being the most effective and positive source of love and discipline possible. Step-parents need to aim higher. The more stable, loving adults a child can have in his or her life the better.

A Co-Parent's Best Investment

Our goal has always been to put each other first, so our children will have the best chance of finding happiness and healthy relationships in adulthood. Since both of us came out of unhealthy marriages with children, being role models has been a primary concern for us and we've wanted to make up for the abusive and negative examples we set for our children before we married each other.

The best investment any co-parent can make is to treat the other biological parent of your children with respect and dignity. Whether still married to you, remarried, or off the grid living on a mountaintop in the Andes and haven't been heard from in years, the most dignified thing you can do for all interested parties is accept, forgive, and not make the parenting struggles any more difficult than they already are.

It will be the basis of a legacy of love for your children when you show them how to love and respect family members.

One wise divorced couple recognized the value of creating a legacy of love for their children, and went about it in a very productive manner. They treated their new arrangement as if it were a business. Andre and Tanya had two children, and divorced after Tanya caught Andre with another woman in one of their beachfront condos in South Florida. Andre was an extremely successful entrepreneur, who was constantly working to build a tremendous fortune and vast business empire. Tanya knew her best bet, to encourage familial love and relationships post-divorce, was to treat their situation in a manner that Andre could respond and identify with. They set up business meetings to discuss family issues, developed long term strategies about how to best provide for their children's future, set up a regular time to speak by phone about the kids, etc.

Eventually both Andre and Tanya remarried. Andre married the woman he was cheating on Tanya with. Both new step-parents embraced the children not as threats but as benefits. Everyone demanded respect of the new people and spouses…..they set aside their egos and insecurities, choosing instead to focus on dignity and the business of co-parenting in a blended family. Their story is beautiful because their values as people and co-parents lead them to marry new spouses who were also committed to honoring the best interests of the children over themselves. And the kids turned out great… both went on to Ivy League universities and topnotch careers.

Legacies of Love

Without a doubt, my children are my best accomplishment, the source of the most joy, and my best contribution to this world. Being a father has been the greatest experience of my life but I've sure made some huge mistakes. These errors I've made are the most regrettable of my life…..by a long shot.

The fact of the matter is our children are watching the movie of our lives unfold before their eyes. What we show them is what they accept as "normal" or routine. Who we are, our values, our character, our words, and our actions, are setting them up for what kind of movie they'll have later in life. What are your core values, those three or four qualities you want your kids, grandkids, and great grandkids to possess? How do you expect them to have those qualities if you don't role model those qualities for them? How are your words and actions teaching them to be the best they can be, lead the happiest and healthiest lives, and learn to raise their own children to be loving and successful people one day?

In my business, most people are worried about what kind of financial inheritance they will leave to their children. We do a lot of settlements which outline exactly what kind of trusts, life insurance, etc. either spouse is obligated to fund for the benefit of children. It's never been easy for me to watch an embittered or enraged spouse spend so much time and money on building their kids' inheritances when they are clueless about the emotional heritage they are leaving as well. I just want to shake them and say, "Their inheritance isn't just about money!"

Generational Awareness

A legacy of love is all about what you want to be known and remembered for as your children watch *The Movie of Your Life*. It will endure through the generations. Love and dignity are the most valuable gifts biological parents, step-parents, or co-parents can provide for their children, but it requires a conscious decision to make it happen.

We need to act now to prepare our children to fulfill their destiny and purpose. Sooner or later, they'll have to make their own decisions, but our character and role modeling supplies them with the proper tools.

The legacy of love is not just about raising good kids and surviving the perils of divorce and blended families. It's about dignity, self-esteem, and integrity. It's about the character of the parents as individuals, the children as individuals, and the character of the family unit across generations. It's about fortifying the integrity of the family so your children's children will have the best possible shot of living a life full of happiness, health, and prosperity. As parents, it's our job to show them the best possible movie of our lives so they will have the strongest legacy on which to live their adulthood.

Mara divorced many years ago and found the courage to really get at the emotional and psychological issues behind her pattern of choosing "bad" or "wrong men". She spent years in therapy digging through her past (which of course means she dignified her past) so she could build toward a better future and marry a man who truly deserved her.

Mara

"My therapist did an amazing job of helping me 'read between the lines' of what was going on in my house when I was growing up. My mother and father had a dysfunctional relationship. She was a total doormat. She never did anything for herself.....it was all for my dad or for me and my sisters. She was always giving and doing and constantly complaining about how exhausted she was."

"As I got older, I learned not to upset her or make her complain any more than she already was. So I started making my own meals, getting my little sisters ready for school, managing homework, and helping my mother take care of my dad. Nobody ever asked or bothered to think about what I needed, or how I could use some support or help. I was just a workhorse for everyone."

"When I got married, this pattern continued. I behaved exactly like my mom except I didn't let my children take over any of the homemaking. But the more I did, the worse I felt. I started getting angry and resentful that nobody was appreciating me as I hoped and longed for."

"My husband certainly didn't appreciate anything. For so many years I comforted myself by feeling morally good about my decision to be the martyr and sacrificial mother willing to do anything for anyone. I started taking anti-depressants to lift my spirits and get more energy to serve, but they didn't really help as much as I'd hoped."

"When my husband left me, I hit bottom. All those years of sacrifice and service for what I thought was a traditional, normal healthy family were for naught."

"My therapist helped me see that I'd become like my mother.....I'd learned from her that it was my 'job' or 'duty' to stay silent about my own needs. I learned that my needs didn't matter, and since I didn't think they mattered, nobody else would either. They all saw me as more of a servant than a woman. My therapist explained that I learned from childhood that 'a good woman' knows not to take care of herself, but to take care of others first."

"I didn't learn anything useful or healthy from my mother because she didn't have anything like that to teach me. She'd given it all away, or had gotten so far removed from the truth of who she was inside, it wasn't accessible for her children to see. There was so little for her to give me emotionally as a little girl, that I had none to give my own kids. And they were seeing my husband take advantage by treating me like dirt. It was pretty scary when I realized that my oldest daughter was turning out the same way."

"It took a while for me to understand the value in my therapist's lessons and advice, because they were so foreign to what I've always been taught, or what most of my friends ascribed to. They also appeared to contradict what my church had taught, until I finally understood things correctly."

"My therapist said if I didn't recognize my needs and act to get them met, nobody would ever, or could ever, satisfy them for me. I had to really get in touch with who I was, and what my needs were, so I could figure out how to meet them and what kind of men I wanted to attract, who would honor me…..needs and all."

"I wanted to get to know who I was, figure out how to be me, and take care of me, so I could really 'give all of me' to my kids and others in a far more effective way. Before, I had only been able to give what little I knew was in there! But now that I see I am a whole person with needs that aren't unreasonable, I can honor myself and others by giving less away. The well is now deep enough and full enough that I don't 'begrudge' anyone what I give them in loving ways. That has been a hard but astonishing lesson for me post-divorce. It's not selfish to recognize and tend to my own needs first! I want to teach this to my kids as part of my legacy of love for them."

I've also seen a lot of women who haven't been able to cope with the demands of motherhood. Parenting is a tough job which deserves to be dignified by responsible, whole people who can be as emotionally fit as possible.

The parents are supposed to be the leaders of the family, and the best leaders aren't personal disasters or basket cases.

Good leaders allocate their resources, manage their time, and know unless their needs are met, they can't adequately serve others. How can you lead and be a good parent when you are sleep-deprived, full of anger, and have no confidence in yourself?

Integrity
One of the keys to healthy self-esteem is integrity – you are who you say you are – your actions reflect your values. It's about being a WHOLE person. You don't hide anything out of fear of what others will think, etc., and this makes you reliable. People can rely on you to do what you say.

We need to teach our children who we are, so they can identify all their sides and develop them. The way we deal with our emotions, health, obstacles in life etc., is how our children learn to deal with theirs in the future. Isn't the goal of every parent to raise children who can deal with life's obstacles, raise healthy families and be happy in their lives?

How can we expect them to achieve all that when we haven't shown them how?

Unfortunately, I had to hit rock bottom in my fatherhood before I could understand where I was going wrong.

Fathers and Integrity / Wholeness
Enjoy your kids! Do fun stuff you all enjoy. Laugh with them. Show your playful side with them. Show your caring, vulnerable side. They look up to you and idolize you much more than you realize. When you are only with them on custody weekends, they are like extra absorbent sponges soaking up everything you do and say, even more because they have less

opportunities to see you. That's why you must be a whole person during the times you do get. You can't just be the weekend warrior dad, doing anything to make them happy like going ice skating or eating loads of junk. You need to invest in their growth and development, not just do the fun stuff so they will "like you".

Manners Matter!
Wow, even at my age, "manners" sounds like a very old-fashioned concept, doesn't it? Yet, if parents don't teach them, our social graces are going to disappear forever, and we will become a society of barbarians. If you weren't taught proper etiquette by your own parents, I strongly urge you to get a book or take a class on the subject. Then start immediately to teach your children.

One of the most obvious ways in which the values of the parents or family are reflected and revealed to others is at the dining table. Parents who do little to teach and encourage their children to demonstrate good manners out of respect for others dining with them, can hardly be expected to turn out dignified, polite, respectful children aware of the rules and reasons for proper etiquette. Do you remember the scene from the movie *Pretty Woman*, where Julia Roberts sits on the table at breakfast rather than properly in a chair, and eats a pancake with her fingers??

That is a perfect picture of her lack of classy behavior vs. Richard Gere's perfect gentleman's manners. What kind of home or family do you think she grew up in?

If you think these things don't matter in today's world, you are dead wrong. Employers in most professions and upper management frequently take their interviewees to lunch or dinner. Why? To observe their table manners and social behavior. To make sure their firm's upscale clients won't be offended by socially unacceptable behavior. A colleague recently told me his firm was looking to hire a recent graduate in the top five percent of his class at the University of Miami School of Law. He related to me that one young man had everything the firm hoped for in a new hire, and they expected to offer him an impressive package to work for them – until they took him to a fancy lunch in downtown Miami. This young man was an Ivy League graduate and a star law student, but he had zero table manners. The firm couldn't afford to hire him if he wasn't presentable to their upscale, high-end clients.

If you want your children to be perceived as ladies and gentlemen, TEACH THEM and require proper behavior from them consistently. Show them what this looks like by modeling it yourselves! Just because the family is no longer "intact", doesn't mean that your values must no longer be intact. It's easy for the demands of single parenting to result in less traditional meals around the table and time constraints to cause oversights on basic demonstrations of proper etiquette such as sending handwritten thank-you notes for gifts.

Children might be disadvantaged in some ways because they aren't from a traditional two-parent home, but teaching them proper etiquette, introductions, handshakes, articulate speech instead of mumbling, eye contact, respect for elders, etc., speaks volumes about the quality of the people who raised them – whether or not they were living under the same roof. You can give them the advantage of teaching them the right way to show others they respect themselves, and those around them, and that they come from an environment where dignified living was honored and valued.

Life Skills
I read a wonderful book years ago that listed all the practical life skills you should teach your kids, and at what ages. You can make your own list, and then please make them practice by giving them age-appropriate regular chores and responsibilities. Your list might start with things such as: How to cook simple meals, How to clean the house, including the bathroom and kitchen, How to do their own laundry, How to change a tire and jump a dead battery, How to handle money and credit cards, How to book a flight.

Every parent, biological, step, or adopted, wants to raise well-adjusted, well-rounded, balanced and happy children who are capable of dealing with everything the world throws at them. I was determined to raise well-mannered, disciplined children who respected their elders. I wanted them to just do what I was telling them to do, and that was exactly how I was treating myself. I was saying to myself, "C'mon Jack! Just keep moving forward. The marriage is over, so get over it and move on. Dealing with your feelings won't make anything better or easier. It won't make up for your past mistakes or the infidelity. So just accept it, and focus on what you can do to be the best person and parent you can be now. Raise these kids right – focus on them, and the rest will take care of itself."

This is what thousands of my clients think too. We all think if we just have our heads screwed on tight and focus on "how to be the best parent possible", our kids will end up achieving the goals we set out for them to achieve – or we hope they will anyway.

The problem with this is that our heads are running the show when our hearts need to be part of the equation as well. In my case, I behaved more like a drill sergeant than a father because I wanted to make sure my children were well-mannered and disciplined. I spent as much time as I could with them because I'd learned from *not* being a constant presence for Stacey, that I couldn't tolerate any more of my kids lacking the knowledge that they had a father who cherished them deeply. I thought I had all of my bases covered and was doing everything right because I was always trying to put them first. *But after 51 years in this business and 30 years to reflect on what was really going on, I now know it's impossible to truly put your children first when you don't truly put yourself first so that you can be the role model they deserve.*

It was easier for me to ignore my sadness and anger, and focus on baseball games, trips to the park, and snowball fights, than dignifying my emotional struggles by paying attention to them. So sure, they knew I was around and took them to do fun things, and paid for stuff, but what was the quality of the product I was working so hard to turn out? How can I expect any higher quality than what I am myself? How can I expect and teach more when I'm not more?

Respect Your Children's Emotional and Psychological Needs

Like most divorcing parents I've represented, I failed to see how neglecting my own emotional and psychological needs made me incapable or ineffective when dealing with those of my children. This is the most important thing I tell parents struggling with denial, resentment, guilt and anger. Parents are the leaders of the family and the best leaders aren't basket cases who are unwilling or unable to do their job properly. When we can't dignify our own needs and deal with our issues, it's almost impossible to help our kids deal with theirs.

Recognize our children have the same emotions as we do. Children are not aliens! They are miniature, undeveloped versions of who they will one day be. They are just like us but in little bodies. This means they experience the same emotions we do in the divorce – fear, resentment, anger, sadness, etc. But when we can't or won't acknowledge our emotions, we struggle with accepting and dealing with theirs.

Whitney

"Both of my parents basically freaked out in their own way during their divorce. One ignored it, and the other collapsed into a big depressed heap. It was terrible to have to go back and forth between their houses with my younger siblings. I had to kind of morph into another person based on the address."

"My Dad ignored it…..he carried on with life, and never discussed my mother or our life before the divorce. He was stoic."

"But Mom was a mess. She gave such conflicting signals about feelings. She always told us we weren't to blame, and she and my dad loved us dearly, but as much as she told us we were all going to be okay, it never was believable. She'd spend most of her day in bed crying, watching 'The Young and the Restless' and old re-runs of 'Mr. Ed'. Mom was just very fragile, and I never felt like I could talk to her about anything I was feeling, either in the divorce or things that were happening at school."

"My therapist told me this is why I'm so disinclined to share or acknowledge my own feelings and it's contributed to the demise of my own marriage. She said I learned from one parent that emotions aren't important enough to admit to having, and from the other I learned if I did acknowledge them, they'd overwhelm me and I wouldn't be able to have a life and function."

"But at the time, I remember feeling so scared all the time. I didn't want to make anything worse for either parent so I just kept my mouth shut at home because I didn't want to burden Mom with my feelings when she couldn't deal with her own. My Dad was no help either. I was desperate to come to him and cry and ask all kinds of questions and talk, but he could never offer much more than a blank stare and then tell me everything would be fine once we went and got ice cream."

Whitney's story is powerful because it shows just how serious the consequences of unhealthy emotional parenting can be, and how the legacy of love is diminished when we don't pay attention to our flaws and make the necessary repairs. But one of the most interesting lessons in her story is what happens when children feel they have no safe place to turn to get their own emotional needs met. Whitney was so aware of her mother's feelings because her actions and functionality were reflective of her emotional status.

Whitney assumed responsibility for her mom's emotions when she declined to "burden" her mother with her own. It is so unfair for children to ever be responsible for a parent in any way. It forces them to grow up before they are ready, but at the same time, it stunts their development and maturity. Rather than developing into emotionally responsible, healthy, balanced adults prepared for a stable happy marriage, they are stunted. Often they are unable to move past where they were when the "responsibility for others" role kicked in.

In Whitney's marriage, she was emotionally undeveloped and had almost no chance of maintaining a healthy marriage where both parties had positive self-esteem. She had shut her emotions completely down at age 13. Her mother taught her to fear them and her dad taught her they didn't really matter. So she wasn't able to cope with them at all. Her emotional immaturity blocked her from sharing any real intimacy with her spouse, and locked her out of any real shot at healthy self-esteem because she was emotionally unaware of herself.

Divorcing with dignity, parenting and self-esteem are all related. When low self-esteem shuts us down and impairs our ability to act in our own best interests, our emotional and psychological divorce can be delayed for years, or is never accomplished. If you have children, you must take responsibly for your emotional health so you can be responsible for theirs. Pay attention to your self-esteem so you can do a better job of paying attention to theirs.

Trapped in the Mistakes of Parenting

I was too ignorant, selfish and hedonistic to be the kind of dad my biological children needed and deserved. I learned my lessons too late, and could only apply those lessons with the children I had left at home to raise – my step-daughters Koula and Maria. Although my relationships with my biological children are better than ever, we've all experienced some rough patches along the way. I am truly blessed with the belief that Stacey, Billy, John and Chris all possess healthy self-esteem, and that legacy could inure to the benefit of their children.

Resentment

It can be a big issue for blended families. Biological children often feel they've been slighted when they see their parent doing a better job raising step-children. I deeply regret these inter-child resentment issues among some of my offspring. I know I'm responsible for it, and I've suffered with guilt for decades. But at some point I learned I wasn't doing them any favors by constantly allowing my guilt to dictate how I treated them. I needed to forgive myself, drop the guilt, and stop trying so hard to make it all up to them. Money and anything else I could think of were my ways of letting them know how sorry I was.

I did the best I could do at the time I was doing it.....and I just had to leave those mistakes in the past and move forward.

Not only does staying trapped in the mistakes of parenting keep you enslaved by the past, it also keeps your children trapped with you. It makes it harder for them to move on and forgive, when we keep reminding them how miserable we were when we missed their birthday party!

Self-Forgiveness

At some point you have to forgive yourself, even when your adult children are unable to move past their own issues about your mistakes. I know many parents who agonize over the guilt of parenting mistakes. Many are punished by their grown children who act out in an attempt to restage the past. If you realize your lack of self-forgiveness is affecting your relationship with your child, and money is a method by which you avoid dealing with these issues, the best thing to do is deal with yourself first before attempting to make drastic changes with your child.

Try to keep communication open. Support them. Cheer them on. And don't make excuses for your behavior now. Don't make promises you can't or won't keep. Try to establish healthy relationships with their spouses.

Respecting Your Children

Divorce and post-divorce are times to get to know everyone again in a new space in life. It's important to respect your children enough to let them heal and adjust to their new lifestyle before introducing them to a stranger who lights you up like a Christmas tree. New relationships after, or God forbid during, divorce can feel so fresh and new. We feel loved and appreciated again and can have a new "spark" to all we do and say. But this can be traumatizing and alienating for children. A child might be forced to experience a completely new kind of parent who complicates his or her adjustment process. When children see mom or dad treating someone new vastly differently from the ex, it brings up all sorts of confusing emotions.

Your kids are trying to adjust to so many changes and they are seeking emotional security and stability in their parents. It's especially hard for children when a fairly absentee parent during marriage shares custody or visitation and includes a new significant other during those times. The children already feel like they weren't important to the absentee parent before the split, and now they really feel like they aren't even worth your undivided attention during the few hours a week you do spend together.

At the same time, a child who is suddenly smothered by a parent who has always seemed like a stranger can struggle to adjust and often feels very used and resentful. One father said, "I think that's what happened with my kids. I behaved so poorly during my marriage because I was never home and when I was, I wasn't involved. To them it appeared as if I were only passing through their lives. I was a joke, a fleeting here-today-gone-tomorrow unreliable nincompoop. I was a daddy of convenience. I wanted to be with them only when it was convenient for me. It had to be on my terms and based on my schedule."

Chapter 9

Integrity

The integrity of your divorce is largely dependent on the integrity of you as a person. It's important to remember this precious gift of divorce done right, because it helps you find peace and satisfaction with your settlement if you "didn't get it all" because you know you endured the ordeal with integrity.

But what is integrity and how does it affect self-esteem? Why is it such an important issue to consider during divorce?

Integrity means truth, reliability, and veracity. It means that you are who you say you are and others can identify your values, needs, or goals simply by watching how you behave. It means that you acknowledge and honor all parts of yourself so that you are an "integrated" human being, and you don't conduct yourself in a manner that honors one of the pieces of self while dishonoring the others.

I represented a true Southern belle once who was incredibly smart and capable of thinking on her own, but her husband didn't allow it. He couldn't tolerate her doing things "her way", or having opinions or needs contrary to his own.

After many years of marriage, she essentially became a puppet and behaved according to what was tolerable for him, regardless of her own self-interests. She told me once, "I think several years into the marriage, I lost all sense of who I was and what I stood for. I tried to save my marriage, but when my self-esteem slowly started to improve, and I understood it's largely built on integrity, I started to see how splintering myself had caused so much damage. For years I was blind to what I really needed, because I was so out of touch with who I was. But once I started 'coming back into who I am', I regained the ability to know what is best for me. I could no longer be married to someone who demanded that I sacrifice who I am for him."

A set of values or principles will provide you with a moral code or compass from which to base your decisions and actions for the rest of your life. Developing a list of values can greatly reduce the confusion, anxiety, and lack of peace we experience in divorce, because it serves as a kind of checklist against which we can evaluate whether certain ideas or decisions are really in our best interest.

It's also important to develop a list of your values when you have no idea who you are in the aftermath of a collapsed marriage. Without knowing who you are, you won't know what you stand for, and all of this will prevent you from getting in touch with your needs, let alone communicating them to others or the person who needs to know this information the most in divorce besides you – your attorney.

Our values and character traits define who we are, and acting on those values shows others we respect ourselves.

When we respect ourselves by holding our values in such high regard we're willing to risk loss of social status or popularity to stick to our principles, and it automatically develops respect from others. Acting on our values shows people we believe in what we stand for, and by endorsing these principles through action, it fortifies our reputation and identity. Even when others might not agree with our principles, it's impossible for them to lack respect for us as a person with the courage of their convictions.

The bottom line is that we tell others how to treat us by how we treat ourselves, and nobody will treat us as honorably as we'd like if our actions are not self-honoring.

Elizabeth was married to a man who thought he was full of integrity but in reality, he had none. Her husband Peter was a pleasure seeker and everything in their marriage was about him and what made him happy. For years, she thought she was living a life of integrity because her actions mirrored her values, and she valued meeting her husband's needs above all else, including her own needs. She clung to this despite Peter's constant trampling of her needs, interests, and desires.

When we discussed integrity, she realized that Peter actually had no integrity because Peter's values were all about self-indulgent pleasures, and his actions were all about materializing those values. He valued wealth, lavish vacations, sexual gratification, fine clothing, building his rare timepiece collection, and keeping his private jet in the divorce. His only aim was to make as much money as possible in life, hobnob with the movers and shakers, and enjoy the hell out of himself – there was nothing he was unwilling to do to achieve these goals or realize these values. But because his values weren't "principles" or character attributes, there was no possibility of conflict between principle and pleasure. He had no risk of losing anything by acting on his "values".

Thinking about your needs makes you more aware of how they aren't being met, which further diminishes self-esteem and builds more resentment toward your spouse. This is why many in oppressive marriages are so broken and self-unaware by the time they divorce. Without any reason to think about these issues in the marriage, they have become greatly alienated from their authentic selves and haven't developed the "muscle" to act in honor of their dignity.

The knowledge that we aren't measuring up to who or what we purport to be is what diminishes self-esteem. It's awful when you put pressure on yourself to be a "good, noble, or loveable person" but your behavior is contrary to those goals. Being who you want to be NOW is your best hope of recovering self-esteem efficiently. The more time you spend acting contrary to your goals and ideals of who you want to be as a human being, the more time you'll spend locked in the hell of low self-esteem and misery.

Divorce – A Wonderful Opportunity to Build Integrity

No matter how you behave in divorce, your behavior reveals much about who you are, so do it the right way. People are really watching at this time in your life – some may be watching to see the trainwreck of your life expecting you to fall apart, and others might watch to see if you truly can redeem yourself and rise from the ashes. Either way, divorce is the opportunity for you to push the reset button on your life and start building a better reputation with yourself, and among others, more than you've ever enjoyed.

The key to integrity is understanding how we accomplish our goals. It is just as important, or even more so, than actually achieving those goals. If we believe that WHO we are as people is more important than what we achieve (i.e., social status, material items, job titles, etc…), it allows us to focus on identifying our values and acting in congruence with them. And this is what living with integrity is all about – identifying your values and behaving in a manner which reflects those values.

Chapter 10

Why I Can't Help Every Client

I can't help those who aren't willing to help themselves. The prospective clients who can't accept my message are often the ones who need to hear it most. They bought this book thinking it would solve all their problems and be the key to finding their "happily ever after". They are most in danger of missing the growth opportunities divorce provides and prefer finger-pointing and blame-shifting to self-examination.

Those with egos downplay the self-esteem issue and think any problems were due to their spouses. They are so invested in elevating themselves through false measures, such as putting down others to build themselves up, that my message and style offends them. They don't like my confrontation.

These are the people who never push rewind or pause. They don't want to look back and learn. They blame others for any bumps in the road and lack the requisite self-responsibility needed to avoid future mistakes.

Not everyone can accept the self-esteem message right away, but I've found that the vast majority of my clients can. If you can accept that it is, or might be a damaged self-esteem which acted as the catalyst in propelling you from your living room to the lawyer's office, you've already achieved the first goal. This will expedite your recovery because you can finally begin to heal what needs healing. If you decide that the marriage might be salvaged by addressing the core self-esteem issues, you have a much better chance of staying together than if you merely addressed the symptoms of the disease.

I confront my receptive clients about the status of their self-esteem. This is how I can figure out where they are in terms of being able to act for themselves – either in saving the marriage, or choosing to divorce. Since they've already told me they want their self-esteem back, they need to understand that staying in a marriage which continues to dissolve any shreds of the self-esteem they still have, does not assist them in recovery.

So if survival instinct is what propels you, then how far are you willing to go to restore that loss? You are already on the road to recovery, but many clients get stuck along the way. That's why I provide a road map and try to assist them when they get bogged down along the way.

The question then becomes, what are you fighting for the survival of? Are you fighting for your marriage to survive, or for yourself to survive? This is a confusing question for many women. Are they fighting for the marriage to survive because they can't survive without it? That's ridiculous. They came into the world unmarried. We all need others to survive and flourish, but it's never healthy when our survival is linked solely to one other, a spouse, a child, a parent, etc. If you think you need your marriage to survive, you are allowing your very survival to be at the mercy of another human being. The survival must be about you.

When I walked off stage that day in September 1961, I wondered what was in store for me. Who would I turn out to be? But I'm an older man now. I know there's more life behind me than in front of me.

I no longer worry about who I'll become. But I am concerned about my clients and their children, and my own children and grandchildren – who will they become? Am I making a meaningful difference in their lives? Will they have the strength to have redemption scenes of their own?

The confrontation with Professor Murray altered the course of my life. What would've happened to me if Professor Murray hadn't taken the time to alert me of my deficiencies before it was too late? Who would I have become? If you've read this book and absorbed any piece of it, you've already alerted yourself to your own deficiencies. My hope is this book was your "Professor Murray Moment", and that your redemption is underway. Some people can't absorb my message or do the work it takes to get themselves back. And for that I am truly sorry – for their movies are destined to be entitled.....

"*Unhappiness Has No Season*"

Made in the USA
Middletown, DE
08 April 2021